GOD, WHERE ARE YOU?!

FINDING STRENGTH & PURPOSE IN YOUR WILDERNESS

My

Bible Project.com ~ You Tube

GOD, WHERE ARE YOU?!

FINDING STRENGTH & PURPOSE IN YOUR WILDERNESS

JOHN BEVERE

USA TODAY BEST-SELLING AUTHOR

God, Where Are You?!
PUBLISHED BY MESSENGER INTERNATIONAL, INC.
610 South Santa Fe Ridge
Palmer Lake, CO 80133
MessengerInternational.org

A previous version of this title was published in 1992 under the title *Victory in the Wilderness*. This updated version offers new and revised content from the author.

Printed in the United States of America.

ISBN 978-1-937558-19-2 (paperback edition)
ISBN 978-1-937558-20-8 (electronic edition)
LCCN: 92090341

Edited by Bruce Nygren, Addison Bevere, Cory Emberson, and Laura Willbur.
Cover design by Allan Nygren.

SPECIAL MARKET SALES
Organizations, churches, pastors, and small group leaders can receive special discounts when purchasing this book and other resources from John Bevere. For more information, please visit www.Messenger International.org, call (800) 648-1477, or send a message to orders@messengerinternational.org.

CONTENTS

FOREWORD

*For the LORD comforts Zion; He comforts all her waste
places and makes her wilderness like Eden, her desert
like the garden of the LORD; joy and gladness will be
found in her, thanksgiving and the voice of song.*

—Isaiah 51:3 ESV

I love the book of Isaiah—he's my favorite Old Testament prophet.
In this particular passage, Isaiah uses imagery to assure us that
God longs to transform our barren expanses into gardens of
life. His words reveal that the arid soil of the desert wastelands
is actually the catalyst of our remaking. The removal of all that
was brings a revelation of what will be. Our Father brings us
through this season of preparation so He can get us *to* our place
of promise.

I had the honor of walking alongside my husband as we tra-
versed deserts of disappointment, where the shifting sands of discouragement threatened to overwhelm us. I watched as he prayed,
reasoned, and cried out, "God, where are You?!"

We stayed up late most nights wondering where we'd gone
wrong. Had there been a misstep or was there some mistake we
could redeem?

Early each morning before sunrise, John would go out to listen and look for these answers . . . hoping that this day would
be the one to bring clarity and a change of scenery. I would wait

anxiously until he returned home. Our sons would be up when he returned.

"Did you hear God say anything?" I'd whisper.

John would shake his head. A sadness would fill my heart and overshadow my hope.

Were we crazy? Had we even heard God? How could we have? If God had led us out to this place, why was He silent in the midst of our desolation?

Yes, I whined in the wilderness.

I only wish I'd known then what I know now. I would have traveled the season with a lighter heart and a faith-filled step. I would have recognized that I was being refined and prepared.

In light of this, I feel this book is a guide and in many ways a gift. Embrace the lessons of this season, and they will serve you well in your next one.

Be encouraged—you are not alone.

—Lisa Bevere

New York Times best-selling author

Co-founder of Messenger International

INTRODUCTION

This book tells of my journey to the wilderness, as well as similar visits of many others. I have not "arrived," nor have I attained all that God would have for me, but it is my prayer that in these pages you will find the strength and courage to press on toward your destiny in God.

I do not claim that this is an exhaustive or all-inclusive study. There is much more that can be written. But this account is from my heart and covers the major aspects of a wilderness season. The intent of this book is to introduce this subject to you, making room for the Holy Spirit to personalize and apply this message to your life.

This book will discuss what the wilderness *is* and what it *is not*—its purpose and benefits. It is my prayer that, by these examples, illustrations, and words of instruction, you will see how to walk wisely in the season of wilderness.

As you read, you'll notice many of my personal examples occurred during my first two positions in ministry. The first was serving my pastor and his guests for four-and-a-half years in Dallas, Texas. My wilderness time came during the last eighteen months in this ministry position. The second occurred during my two-and-a-half years of being a youth pastor at a church in Florida. The wilderness I experienced in this position made the first desert season in Dallas seem like a picnic. Oddly enough, this intense desert also spanned the last eighteen months of that tenure.

Have there been other wilderness seasons in my life? Yes. But by the time they arrived, I had already come into a greater understanding of what they represented. So, consequently, I wasn't crying out repeatedly, "God, what's going on?" or "God, where are You?!" I had learned enough in the previous seasons to know what was happening and what was the appropriate response.

I've talked with countless men and women who are in the midst of this season. In our conversations, I usually hear about confusion and frustration. So many are clueless as to what's going on. In fact, my wife, Lisa, and I did two podcasts on this subject recently, and the response to this topic was the greatest we'd ever had. This caused me to relook at the first book I ever wrote, initially published as *Victory in the Wilderness*.

I wrote that book nearly thirty years ago. In carefully rereading it, I realized it was a prophetic message more appropriate for the late 1980s and early 1990s. So, my editor and I extracted the timeless truths, added numerous insights gleaned in the past thirty years, and did a complete rewrite. So this is not an updated and revised book, but rather a fresh, new message. I believe that the book you're holding is now a timeless message that will help people—both now and in the generations to come—navigate this important season.

We are told, "To everything there is a season, A time for every purpose under heaven" (Ecclesiastes 3:1 NKJV). There are seasons in our lives, and every season has a purpose. It is important to understand the purpose of the season in order to act correctly. It would be interesting if a man wearing his snowsuit got on a chairlift and rode up a mountain with his snowboarding gear, only to fall flat on his face when getting off the chairlift. Why? It's summertime and there isn't any snow! His actions are beneficial for wintertime, but are detrimental in his current season.

In this book it's my intent to share the understanding of this important season of pruning and strengthening. Its purpose: *preparation.* You'll quickly observe that I discuss much in regard to ministry. All of us are called, some to the marketplace, some to the educational field, some to healthcare, some to government, and the list goes on. My calling is the fivefold ministry, so my stories reflect this. However, the principles apply no matter what arena of life God has called you to. Those in the marketplace need preparation time for their calling, just as ministers of the gospel do. And this is true for all other arenas of life.

One other detail: I've included some bonus content in the book entitled "Survival Tips for Your Journey." These are brief, standalone insights and words of encouragement relevant to making your time in the wilderness as productive as possible. It is my hope that this message will bring clarity, so you don't have to suffer from the ignorance of the season as I did, and to encourage you in your continued pursuit of Him who alone satisfies.

Most sincerely,

John Bevere

January 2019

1

"WHERE
ARE YOU?"

*extreme barreness
need bitterness   levelheadedness*

*When we suffer aridity and desolation with equanimity,
we testify our love to God; but when He visits us with the
sweetness of His presence, He testifies His love to us.*

—Madame Guyon / Jeanne-Marie Bouvier de la Motte-Guyon

*Look, I go forward, but He is not there and backward,
but I cannot perceive Him; When He works on the left
hand, I cannot behold Him; When He turns to the right
hand, I cannot see Him.*

—Job 23:8–9 (NKJV)

was angry at everybody. And really not sure why.

Nothing seemed to go right.

Our firstborn son, Addison, was eighteen months old—I was impatient with him.

I was yelling at my wife, Lisa.

I was disappointed with my pastor.

I was upset with the people I worked with.

If I would have been honest about it, I was probably disappointed and offended with God too. I whined, "What are You doing?"

"Why aren't You moving in my life?"

"Where is the fulfillment of Your promises to me?"

"Why are things so wrong?"

"Why are You not talking to me?"

Over and over I found myself muttering this lame complaint, "Where *are* You?"

Have you ever had a time when it seemed like the Lord was so close that all you had to do was whisper His name and He was *right there* and answered *right then?*

But then the time came when you sent Him one message after another, but there was no response. He seemed to have totally disappeared from your life. Maybe that's where you are now and your question, which you want to shout into the stillness, is the same one I was asking: "God, where are You?!"

I was in the wilderness, but I didn't know it. I was living in Dallas, Texas, and thought I was a good follower of Jesus who had been forgotten by God. As a young Christian, I think it was my first true visit to the wilderness.

Before this, all I had needed to do was cry out and the Lord would instantly respond. I remember Him quickly answering the most trivial of requests. His presence was so near, evident, and strong. Now, I just could not figure out what was happening. I was on my knees, day after day, crying out, "God, what is going on? It seems like You are a million miles away!"

I kept reviewing my life and asking, "What terrible sin have I committed?"

Well, the truth was, of course, that like every person on the planet, I periodically slipped into sin, but I was also quickly repenting and asking for the forgiveness Jesus offers. To my knowledge, there was not some persistent, willful sin in my life.

"God, why aren't You talking to me anymore?" I asked on one dry day after another.

I certainly was not in the same league with that great man of the Bible, Job, but I was having some of the same reactions. Job's words, which used to seem foreign, were now making sense. Some of the verses expressed these feelings so well of what seemed like wilderness abandonment:

"Look, I go forward, but He is not *there*,
And backward, but I cannot perceive Him;

When He works on the left hand, I cannot behold *Him;*
When He turns to the right hand, I cannot see *Him*."
(Job 23:8–9 NKJV)

I kept on praying, but the heavens seemed like brass.

Then the Lord showed me that the Christian life has some parallels to how a child grows up. I had been a spiritual infant, but now I was moving to a new stage. At the time I had a great natural example in front of me. Addison was about eighteen months old. Lisa was a great mother, so when Addison whimpered, she was right there to care for him. In a flash he would be in her arms, enjoying the sustenance and comfort as he breastfed.

But then Addison, as does every child, needed to grow toward maturity. With all of our boys—we have four—the time came when they needed to feed themselves. Oh my, what a mess—you've seen it! They try to eat and half the food is all over the high chair and the floor.

Children get so frustrated that *you* won't feed them like in the past, but what you are doing is being a responsible mother or father. When our sons were flinging the food around, we wanted to jump in and take over, yet we knew it would hinder their progress. We were allowing our boys to grow up. We certainly didn't want to end up still spoon-feeding one of them when he was eighteen!

As babies grow, the level of assistance they receive changes to encourage growth and development. God does a similar thing with us so we can develop and mature spiritually. When we are newly born again and filled with His Spirit, for a season He manifests Himself at our every cry. But then, after time passes—and hopefully we move beyond just wanting milk (Hebrews 5:12)—in order to help us grow up and mature, He allows us to go through times in which He does not respond instantly to our every call.

When the Lord helped me understand that growing in spiritual maturity was something like the process every person must experience from childhood to adulthood, I became more reflective and wondered, *Have I been wrong? Is what I'm going through not some kind of punishment from the Lord? Is it possible that I've been led to the wilderness to learn something—to grow in some way that will make me better equipped to follow and serve Jesus?*

Then I recalled that this is *exactly* what had happened to Jesus. Almost immediately after John baptized Him and His Father praised Him, Jesus was escorted by the Holy Spirit to the wilderness. He wasn't being reprimanded, and He certainly had not committed any sin.

So during my angry pity party, the thought eventually hit: *So, maybe this wilderness experience is not as awful as I'm making it?*

Perception of the Wilderness

If we are to be like Jesus, our character must develop. And to a great extent, the wilderness is God's choice place for this to happen. And often while we are there, God appears to be miles away and His promises seem empty. But that's only how it feels and isn't reality. In truth, He is close at hand, for He has promised never to leave nor forsake us (Hebrews 13:5 NKJV).

The wilderness is a time when you appear to be going in the opposite direction of your dreams and the promises you once were certain He'd made to you. In the wilderness you sense no spiritual growth and development. In fact, you may feel you are regressing. His presence seems to diminish, rather than grow. You may even feel unloved and ignored. But you are not.

Indeed, the wilderness is a common destination for sincere Christ followers—although when you visit there, you may feel very alone. The truth is, the wilderness is a necessary destination for every child of God. In fact, to progress toward a healthy maturity as a disciple of Jesus, you may have several journeys through the wilderness.

I wish I could tell you that you could select a Google Map route that would show you a shortcut or detour around this barren place, but there isn't one. And, my friend, that is a good thing, because the journey through the wilderness—our acceptance of this time or season—is necessary if we are to make it to our promised land!

Just What Is the Wilderness?

Thankfully, most of us have not actually had to survive physically in a barren place, such as a real desert where there's very little water and shelter is hard to find. The days are hot, the nights cold, and we are alone, thirsty, and hungry. On top of it, we are lost and have no idea how to find our way out. We may not have undergone that experience, but we have had the *emotions* of the wilderness. In this book, I will share some key incidents from my own wilderness visits—I've had a number of them and not one was a picnic!

The good news is that the wilderness does not have to be a negative time if we are eager to obey God. I know this sounds counterintuitive, but the desert's purpose is quite positive: to train, purify, strengthen, and prepare us for a new move of His Spirit, resulting in us becoming more fruitful.

Unknowingly, when entering the wilderness, many people panic and behave unwisely. Without understanding, they search for, and do, the wrong things. An example might be a radical change in a career or changing from one church to another—any drastic move in their life that they think will bring happiness or restore what was normal. For a single person, it might be leaping into a new relationship after the hurt of a painful breakup.

If you search for an escape route before understanding why God has you in a particularly dry situation, you unwittingly will prolong your wilderness time. This may cause more hardship, frustration, and even defeat, because you don't understand the season or the place to which God has led you.

This was the case with the children of Israel during their forty years in the wilderness. A lack of understanding of what was happening to them caused an entire generation to be unfit to inherit the Promised Land. How tragic! God's purpose in leading them to the wilderness was to test, train, and prepare them to be mighty warriors able to capture and occupy their divine promise—a new homeland. But instead, the children of Israel erroneously perceived the wilderness as punishment; so they murmured, complained, and lusted constantly.

When the time came for them to leave the wilderness and conquer and occupy the Promised Land, after their spies returned and gave the intelligence briefing, the people heeded the evil report of the murmurers and complainers. Given the choice between God's promises and ability and man's perceptions and inability, they chose to believe man rather than God. They bought the lie that they were going to suffer defeat and not receive their land flowing with milk and honey. Their ignorance of God's nature and character caused them to act wickedly.

So God said in so many words, "Okay, have it your way." What was to have been a brief wilderness journey of one year became a lifetime experience.

Ouch! You and I don't want a decision like that on our resume! But we can learn from their mistakes, as the apostle Paul points out: "These things happened to them as examples, and they were written for our instruction" (1 Corinthians 10:11 CSB).

If we can learn to recognize when we have entered a wilderness experience, instead of gritting our teeth and complaining, we can be thankful, knowing that beyond this place is a "promised land" of new maturity, power, blessings, opportunity, and fulfilled promises. Wouldn't that make the hard times not so hard? We will then agree with James, who writes:

> When troubles of any kind come your way, consider it an opportunity for great joy. . . . For when your endurance is fully developed, you will be perfect and complete, needing nothing. (James 1:2, 4)

Does a Wilderness Visit Mean I've Really Messed Up?

Good question!

It makes sense that many of us, when we are in a wilderness season, will ask, "What have I done wrong? How did I so displease

God?" This is a misunderstanding of the meaning or purpose of the wilderness.

In the Bible and throughout history, men and women have

Survival Tips for Your Journey

#1 Understand Your Time

Most of us are surprised by the wilderness. God is so good and we grow accustomed to His blessings, presence, and promises. We just never expect the good times to cease. But then one day, we realize that something has shifted. So rather than panicking, it's important to step back and gain some perspective. You need to understand what you're going through, because if you don't understand the season and where you are, then you'll respond incorrectly.

It would be like moving from a southern Florida climate to northern Canada. When winter comes and the thermometer drops way down to the negative temperatures, it's good to know where you are or you might go outside without a coat!

The same thing applies in the wilderness. If you don't pay attention to the clues that signal a stay in a barren place, you will experience a lot of frustration and may even make a costly mistake. In the Old Testament we read that the sons of Issachar "understood the times and knew what Israel should do" (1 Chronicles 12:32 NET).

When you understand your time in the wilderness, you'll also know what to do.

found the wilderness to be a time of preparation for their destiny in God. So the wilderness is not God's rejection but His place of preparation.

I do think that it's certainly possible to end up in a dry place in life as a result of bad choices. The truth is that no matter how far we have come in being like Jesus, we still have sin to deal with and have the potential to mess up. So, it's possible that a really bad decision or a series of not-so-great choices can put us in a ditch.

But here's the truth of the matter: We have a forgiving God and a great High Priest who understands our weaknesses. So the first step of getting out of that ditch, or maybe heading toward the exit of the self-inflicted wilderness, is to go to our loving Father and say, "Dad, I have sinned by _____ (fill in the blank). Please forgive me. I repent of this sin, and now by Your grace, I will live differently."

So, what I'm saying is that even if you are in a barren place in your life because of some mistakes, get right with the Lord and let Him accomplish what He wants to teach you and move on—hopefully out of the desert sooner rather than later. Of course, the timing is up to Him; the Psalmist writes, "My times are in Your hand" (Psalm 31:15 NKJV). Having said all that, though, it's most likely you are in the wilderness because it's the precise place God wants you now. You've made no mistakes to bring you to this place of hardship. I know, in some ways that makes this experience even harder to deal with. That's one of the main reasons I'm writing this book—to help you understand how God views the wilderness and how much He wants to use it to help us grow and become more like Jesus!

Another point that must be understood clearly is that God

didn't bring you to the wilderness to abandon you to Satan's devices and forget about you. Before the second-generation children of the Exodus were allowed to enter the Promised Land, God reminded them:

> "Remember how the LORD your God led you through the wilderness for these forty years, humbling you and testing you to prove your character, and to find out whether or not you would obey His commands." (Deuteronomy 8:2)

So even though the Israelites had really messed up and way overstayed in the wilderness because of their foolishness, ingratitude, and rebellion—God was going to turn it all into something good! That's what He does—I'm so glad! Aren't you?

Don't be misinformed—the Lord does not stop working in our lives just because we are in the wilderness. He leads us *through* it; without Him, we could never make it through. Furthermore, it is *not* a place in which we are put on a shelf until He desires to use us. That is not the way our compassionate Father operates. On the contrary, it is a place and time during which He works mightily.

You may be familiar with the expression, "You can't see the forest for the trees." Well, the wilderness is much the same—it is difficult to see God moving when you are in the midst of it.

This important truth must be clearly stated: the wilderness is not a place of defeat, at least not to those who obey God. Jesus, weak from hunger, with no human in whom to confide or to receive encouragement, and without physical comfort or supernatural manifestation for forty days, was attacked by the devil in the wilderness. Jesus defeated him with the Word of the Lord! The wilderness is not a time when God's children are defeated: "But thanks be to God who always leads us in triumphal procession in Christ . . ." (2 Corinthians 2:14 NET).

While the people of Israel sojourned in the wilderness, they were harassed by the nations of that area. The Lord told Israel to fight back. The children of Israel defeated the Amorites (Numbers 21:21–25), the Midianites (Numbers 31:1–11), and the people of Bashan (Numbers 21:33–35). If God's purpose was for them to experience defeat, He would not have told them to defend their position. Although it wasn't intended as a time of defeat, most died without entering the Promised Land. This was not the way God desired it to be but, rather, the sad result of their disobedience.

I hope this settles in your heart that the reason behind the wilderness is not the disapproval or punishment of God. Nor is it a place in which God abandons and forgets about you. Nor is it a place where we lie down and accept defeat!

God Is Up to Something Good!

The wilderness is not a time for seeking signs, blessings, abundance, or wonders, but a time to seek the heart of God, which will produce character and strength in you. It is a time to maintain vision. Otherwise, without the clear view of the promise in our hearts, this time will seem discouraging and can foster complaining.

If there is an understanding of your position in life, it brings your life into perspective. Then you can see God's hand, even when you may not feel His touch. It is a time when your love for Him matures beyond "What will He do to benefit me?" and turns to "What does He desire of me?"

Earlier I touched on the frustration that the ancient saint Job expressed; how he just could not grasp what God was doing. No matter where he turned, he could not find God! If that were the end of Job's analysis, it would be a real downer. But Job did not give up in despair and offered these words of faith and hope:

"But He knows the way that I take; When He has tested me, I shall come forth as gold." (Job 23:10 NKJV)

What a breathtaking insight! As hard as we try to figure out where God is taking us, He knows the way. We can trust Him completely, because as the apostle Paul writes, "I'm fully convinced that the One who began this glorious expression of grace in you will faithfully continue the process of maturing you through your union with Him and will complete it" (Philippians 1:6 TPT).

And we know that's the truth . . . even in the wilderness.

2

GOOD COMPANY

As Christians face storms of adversity, they may rise with more beauty. They are like trees that grow on mountain ridges—battered by winds, yet trees in which we find the strongest wood.

—Billy Graham

Then Jesus, being filled with the Holy Spirit . . . was led by the Spirit into the wilderness.

—Luke 4:1 (NKJV)

W elcome to the wilderness! Are you surprised by such a cheerful greeting? Normally, we don't expect that spending some time in a spiritual desert is a good thing, but you need to know that our beloved Father has a high regard for such places and you are now in good company.

If you think the wilderness might be a good site not to visit on your journey of faith, I urge you to reconsider! The truth is that in the wilderness we find the footprints of countless saints—even the Son of God—who have spent significant time on visits here.

In other words—when we go to the wilderness, we are in good company . . . and not alone.

Please don't accuse me of name-dropping, but the list of wilderness dwellers is pretty impressive.

Of course I've already mentioned Job, the man whom the Bible describes as "the greatest of all the people of the East" (Job 1:3 NKJV). He lost everything—his possessions, children, health, the support of his wife. A splendid, righteous man, Job was also accused of secret sins by close friends. Job was so despondent in his wilderness that he said it would have been better if he'd never been born.

In the wilderness you walk where Abraham, a wealthy man

from Ur who was settled in comfort, was asked by God to leave everything behind and begin a journey to find a new promised land. And Sarah was right there with him step by step! Much of their journey was spent in deserts.

Moses was very familiar with the wilderness. He had been raised in Pharaoh's court as a prince, but after killing an Egyptian, he found himself on the backside of the desert, watching sheep for forty years, which is where Moses was when God revealed Himself in the burning bush:

> One day Moses was tending the flock of his father-in-law, Jethro, the priest of Midian. He led the flock far into the wilderness and came to Sinai, the mountain of God. There the angel of the LORD appeared to him in a blazing fire from the middle of a bush. Moses stared in amazement. Though the bush was engulfed in flames, it didn't burn up. "This is amazing," Moses said to himself. "Why isn't that bush burning up? I must go see it." When the LORD saw Moses coming to take a closer look, God called to him from the middle of the bush, "Moses! Moses!" "Here I am!" Moses replied. (Exodus 3:1–4)

Then, as we know, Moses went back to Egypt and led his people out of Egypt into—why of course—the wilderness!

In the wilderness you encounter Joseph, the highly favored son of his father who was thrown in a pit by his own brothers, then sold as a slave and trafficked to Egypt. Later he was put in prison, after being framed for a crime he didn't commit. There, in Pharaoh's dungeon, God revealed Himself to Joseph and he began to interpret the dreams of the baker and the butler. It unknowingly prepared him to interpret the dream of Pharaoh himself.

And then there's King David. Samuel prophesied that he would be the next king, yet shortly afterward, David found himself preparing for the throne by dwelling in caves and wandering in the wilderness. There, God revealed Himself to David as his Shepherd, his Strength, his Shield, his Fortress.

John the Baptist was called to be a great prophet—his dad had told him of the vision that revealed this. Yet it was in the wilderness, not in a Bible school, that the Lord revealed Himself to John, who ended up living in the deserts of Judea, wearing animal skins and eating insects. Luke 3:2–3 says, ". . . the Word of God came unto John the son of Zacharias in the wilderness. And he came into all the country about Jordan, preaching the baptism of repentance for the remission of sins" (KJV).

It was in the wilderness of Arabia that God revealed the mysteries of what would become much of the New Testament to the apostle Paul, who writes that it was God's purpose "to reveal His Son to me so that I would proclaim the Good News about Jesus to the Gentiles. When this happened, I did not rush out to consult with any human being. Nor did I go up to Jerusalem to consult with those who were apostles before I was. Instead, I went away into Arabia . . . ." (Galatians 1:16–17).

Where was John the apostle when he received *The Revelation of Jesus Christ*?

I, John, am your brother and your partner in suffering
and in God's Kingdom and in the patient endurance to
which Jesus calls us. I was exiled to the island of Patmos for

preaching the Word of God and for my testimony about
Jesus. (Revelation 1:9)

Patmos was a deserted island—a perfect spot for a wilderness
experience.

Most importantly, you are accompanied by Jesus, who after
receiving the blessing in public of His Father and the Holy Spirit,
was divinely sent into the wilderness to face Satan's temptations.

I have observed that this is often the pattern: God shows us
great things that He intends to do through us in the future, and
then He leads us straight into a wilderness to prepare us.

If the wilderness was required for great saints and our Lord
Jesus, then I can grasp the idea that it will be good for me to spend
some time in the desert, although I may certainly wish there were
an easier path. The wilderness is the place where God tests, humbles, strengthens, and refines us. This is where He molds godly
character in us. It is the preparation ground for future fruitful work
in His kingdom.

The most exciting thing about the wilderness is that it is the
place where God reveals Himself in fresh new ways! The prophet
Isaiah writes:

> For the LORD shall comfort Zion: He will comfort all her waste
> places; and He will make her wilderness like Eden, and her des-
> ert like the garden of the LORD; joy and gladness shall be found
> therein, thanksgiving, and the voice of melody. (Isaiah 51:3 KJV)

The Garden of Eden was where God revealed Himself to
Adam and they had fellowship there.

In the wilderness you become hungry and thirsty for the Lord. Therefore, when God gets ready to reveal Himself, in your deprived and more-focused state, you can more easily turn away from the things of this life and turn toward Him. If we are to respond to God's call for us, our experience will be like this. It's in the wilderness that the Lord reveals Himself to us in a fresh way. Isaiah 45:15 says, "Truly You *are* God, who hide Yourself, O God of Israel, the Savior!" (NKJV) For those who deeply desire Him, He does this to create a greater hunger for the ecstasy of intimate fellowship. The Lord also hides Himself from those who are not

---

Survival Tips for Your Journey

#2 No Matter How Lonely You Feel, God Is Present

Often a significant wilderness experience is what seems to be the total absence of God! Just when you seem to need to sense His presence the most, He seems a million miles away.

It's important that you understand the two manifestations of God's presence. The first one is based on these words from Scripture, "I will never leave you nor forsake you" (Hebrews 13:5 NKJV). This is the omnipresence of God. It's what King David refers to: "If I ascend into heaven, You are there; If I make my bed in hell, behold, You are there" (Psalm 139:8 NKJV). If you believe what Scripture says and you trust God, then the reality is that no matter how you feel or what happens, God is with you.

Dealing with Wilderness:
1) Withdraw GOOD COMPANY 25
2) Pray, 3) Bring friends into
support you in prayer

hungry for Him. He will not be taken for granted. He will never be regarded as ordinary.

We don't know God, we know ~~him~~ about him.

Hungry for God

To those who seek and search for God with all their heart, He will reveal Himself.

Remember, God said that He brought the children of Israel into the wilderness to humble them and cause them to hunger. However, instead of hungering for God as Joshua did, the people

---

The other presence of God, which all of us love and is also a part of the Christian life, is the manifest presence. To "manifest" means to bring out of the unseen and into the seen, out of the unheard and into the heard, out of the unknown and into the known. It's when God makes Himself real to our actual physical senses. It's wonderful to enjoy this encounter, which can happen during worship, private prayer, on a walk through the forest, in common activities of daily life—in perhaps an infinite number of ways.

So when you are spiritually hungry and thirsty in the wilderness, if God doesn't come and bless you with His beautiful, breathtaking presence, just relax and *lean into His promises*—the main one being, "I will never leave you nor forsake you." When we celebrate Him in the absence of His manifest presence, it communicates even louder our unfailing love for Him.

hungered for the things that the Lord had removed from them. So when He came to reveal Himself to them, as He had done with Moses, they had no appetite for Him. In fact, they rejected Him. In Deuteronomy, we read:

> "But when you heard the voice from the heart of the darkness, while the mountain was blazing with fire, all your tribal leaders and elders came to me. They said, 'Look, the LORD our God has shown us His glory and greatness, and we have heard His voice from the heart of the fire. Today we have seen that God can speak to us humans, and yet we live! But now, why should we risk death again? If the LORD our God speaks to us again, we will certainly die and be consumed by this awesome fire. Can any living thing hear the voice of the Living God from the heart of the fire as we did and yet survive? Go yourself and listen to what the LORD our God says. Then come and tell us everything He tells you, and we will listen and obey.'" (Deuteronomy 5:23–27)

Again, God desired to reveal Himself to them in the wilderness, as He had done with Moses, but they backed off and made this request to Moses: "You go and speak to the Lord and come to us and tell us all that He says and we will do it."

Sadly, the people never did *know* God, they only knew *about* Him. Therefore, they never could do as He commanded them. Because of not knowing Him, they never saw the land that was promised to them and they died in the wilderness.

When God brings us into a wilderness, as He did with John,

Moses, David, Joseph, Paul, and others, it will be to test us, to see if we will hunger for Him or if we will hunger for the comforts and pleasures that have eluded us. James writes:

> And even when you ask, you don't get it because your motives are all wrong—you want only what will give you pleasure. You adulterers! Don't you realize that friendship with the world makes you an enemy of God? I say it again: If you want to be a friend of the world, you make yourself an enemy of God. Do you think the Scriptures have no meaning? They say that God is passionate that the Spirit He has placed within us should be faithful to Him. And he gives grace generously. As the Scriptures say, "God opposes the proud but gives grace to the humble." So humble yourselves before God. Resist the devil, and he will flee from you. Come close to God, and God will come close to you. Wash your hands, you sinners; purify your hearts, for your loyalty is divided between God and the world. (James 4:3–8)

When we draw near to God by seeking Him with all our heart, then He will draw near to us. The children of Israel were more interested in their own desires (lusts) than in God's. They were adulterers and adulteresses, seeking the comfort and security that the world's ways could bring them. They soon forgot that all these luxuries and provisions couldn't save the Egyptians or their army.

God says that in order to draw near to Him, we must do two things. First, we must cleanse our hands. Second Corinthians 7:1 says, "Having therefore these promises, dearly beloved, let us cleanse ourselves from all filthiness of the flesh and spirit, perfecting holiness in the fear of God" (KJV). Sin separates us from God: "But your iniquities have separated you and your God and your sins have hid His face from you, so that you will not hear" (Isaiah 59:2 NKJV).

Second, we must purify our hearts. The key to this is what James says, "Purify your hearts, you double-minded" (4:8 NIV). Double-minded people fluctuate back and forth from the Spirit to the flesh. They have not set their mind and affections on the things of God. Colossians 3:1–2 says, "If then you were raised with Christ, seek those things which are above, where Christ is, sitting at the right hand of God. Set your mind on things above, not on things on the earth" (NKJV).

What you diligently seek is what your affections are set upon. The key word is *set*. When a woman has her hair permed, each hair is chemically altered and set in curls. Now she has curly hair because each strand has been set. You can pull that hair straight, but when the tension is released it will bounce back to where it was set.

People can go to church, sing on the worship team, and participate in Christian activities, but where is their mind when they are not doing something "Christian"? It will be where it is set. As soon as the person leaves the church building or Christian atmosphere, their mind will bounce back to what it is set on, just like that permed hair bounces back.

I've talked with many in churches around the country who sing the worship songs, take notes on their phone during the messages, and even give their time to the church's various ministries. These are not bad things, of course, but in between the church services and volunteer opportunities, all they discuss is money, professional sports, clothes, what's new on social media, hobbies, the opposite sex, food, shopping experiences, favorite phone apps, and other things of the world. They light up when discussing those things, but reading the Bible, praying, reaching out to minister to others, and even going to church are things they do out of obligation.

When a man falls in love with a woman and gets engaged to be married, you don't have to tell that man to think and talk about her. She's on his mind constantly, and there's a spark in his voice as he says her name. The reason is that his affection, or heart, is set on her. His mind is not double. He is not thinking about other women. He is in love!

David says in Psalm 16:8, "I have set the LORD always before me" (NKJV). His mind was not double. His heart was pure. He did not have other things in his heart that he loved as he loved the Lord. His love for God far overshadowed any good thing this world had to offer. Things that we love, like, or trust in more than Jesus are called idols. David writes:

Who may ascend into the hill of the LORD? Or who may stand in His holy place? He who has clean hands and a pure heart, Who has not lifted up his soul to an idol, Nor sworn deceitfully. (Psalm 24:3–4 NKJV)

The person who does not love, like, or trust in anything or anyone more than Jesus is the one who has a pure heart. Jesus says in Matthew 10:37, "'If you love your father or mother more than you love Me, you are not worthy of being Mine; or if you love your son or daughter more than Me, you are not worthy of being Mine.'"

In the time of the wilderness, let us not be as the children of Israel, who loved their earthly lives so much that they missed their opportunity to know God.

Isaiah 35:1–2 says:

Even the wilderness and desert will be glad in those days.
   The wasteland will rejoice and blossom with spring
      crocuses. Yes, there will be an abundance of flowers
   and singing and joy!
The deserts will become as green as the mountains of Lebanon,
   as lovely as Mount Carmel or the Plain of Sharon.
There the LORD will display His glory,
   the splendor of our God.

It is in the wilderness that the glory of the Lord is revealed!

Let's join the company of all the great saints who have gone before us! Let us draw near to God with clean hands and a pure heart, as David, Moses, Paul, Joseph, and other great men and women of God have done!

3

THE NECESSARY WILDERNESS

Soar back through all your own experiences. Think of how the Lord has led you in the wilderness and has fed and clothed you every day. How God has borne with your ill manners, and put up with all your murmurings and all your longings after the "sensual pleasures of Egypt"! Think of how the Lord's grace has been sufficient for you in all your troubles.

—Charles H. Spurgeon

The LORD your God led you . . . in the wilderness, to humble you and to test you, to know what was in your heart . . .

—Deuteronomy 8:2 (NKJV)

F or me, that first visit to the wilderness was a complete shock. Honestly, my first couple of years as a follower of Christ were like an extended honeymoon. Lisa and I had settled in Dallas, Texas, and after some time working as an engineer, I took a ministry position with our church. I was given the "job" of serving my pastor and his wife and helping host the guest speakers at our large church. What a joy! I thought I was in heaven. I was taking care of the greatest ministers of the gospel on the planet, because our church was one of the most well-known in America.

As these great national and international leaders arrived at the airport, I was there to pick them up and drive them to the church or to where they were staying. During their visits, I always drove them where they needed to go and shared meals with them. I got to spend hours and hours with some of the greatest people in ministry of our generation. My first years in this position were fantastic—full of life.

But then things started getting tough. Really, really tough. I didn't know it at the time, because God hadn't revealed it to me, but I was entering a wilderness. This is where God trains us. This is where our character is developed and our faith is strengthened. A necessary wilderness.

Picture this: You are an Israelite, recently freed after a lifetime of slavery. You just experienced the frightening, yet exhilarating, walk between two walls of swirling, angry waters to come out safe and dry on the other side. You turned to watch as those same walls that gave protection to you closed in on your enemies. Your tormentors were destroyed, forever gone! You joyously celebrated and danced at God's victorious deliverance! You feel invincible, knowing that God is on your side. You will never doubt His might or faithfulness again!

But now the scene is different: it is a few days later—you are tired, thirsty, and hot. You are not at the threshold of the "promised" land; instead, you are wandering aimlessly in a desert filled with serpents and scorpions. You are no longer dancing and singing to the Lord about the horse and its rider thrown into the sea, but complaining to your leader saying, "Why have you brought us out of Egypt? To kill us and our children and our livestock with thirst?"

Now, let's look at you . . . do you believe God mightily delivered you from the power of the enemy only to leave you wandering aimlessly and indefinitely through a desert of confusion and silence? Was this His purpose? Of course not—this is just a necessary place to visit on your way to a promised place.

Just as the Lord led the children of Israel out of Egypt into the wilderness, so He leads you. The devil did not lead you here, God did. And there is a purpose—a divine plan—for this dry time. First, He humbles us, then He tests us. He does this so we can know the *true* nature of our hearts.

How does He humble? "So He humbled you, allowed you to hunger, and fed you with manna" (Deuteronomy 8:3 NKJV). He humbled the Israelites by allowing them to hunger. But His next statement declares He fed them with manna. It sounds contradictory. How could He cause them to hunger while feeding them manna?

Now, manna is the best food you can eat—it is on the menu of the angels! Elijah was strengthened for a forty-day journey on just two cakes of it. And the Israelites had an abundance of it. They received a fresh shipment from heaven six mornings a week, and on this sixth morning the manna miraculously lasted through the seventh day. *They never missed a meal* from the day God first gave them manna until they camped on the shores of the Promised Land.

So why did God say, "I caused you to hunger?" What hunger is He speaking of? To understand, consider their situation. Let's say all you had for breakfast was a loaf of bread, and every evening all you had for dinner was a loaf of bread. No butter, no peanut butter, no jelly, no cold cuts, no tuna fish, *just bread*. Now, we're not just talking about a few days or weeks, but *forty years* of this diet!

When I was a youth pastor, we took fifty-six young people to the nation of Trinidad for an eight-day mission trip. The church in Trinidad prepared our meals, and our hosts were most gracious. But every day we ate chicken. They prepared it many different ways and served it with rice and vegetables, but it was *always chicken*.

After eight days of chicken, we hungered for something else. Upon returning home, one of the young men in our group asked his mother what was for dinner, and she replied, "Chicken!" He cried out and then begged her to take him for a hamburger.

In Trinidad we were privately whining after only eight days;

can you imagine forty years? Not four years but *forty* years of the exact same food! We now see how God caused them to hunger. He didn't give them the things their appetite wanted but what they really needed to stay alive and healthy.

What else about their circumstances caused them to hunger, to long for what they didn't have? When we read this story we might think it's quite remarkable that their clothes and shoes didn't wear out—what a savings to the family budget. Well, how would you like to wear the same wardrobe for forty years? How boring! No trips to a shopping mall or checking out new styles online. The same pair of brown sandals for forty years!

Yes, they had their basic needs provided for—protection from heat and cold—but so much of what they wanted was missing.

And think of the monotony of the same scenery, day after day—not for a few weeks, but for *forty years*. How would we like to see the same cactus, bulrushes, parched ground—no peaceful streams, lush forests, scenic vineyards, or beautiful lakes—just desert day after day?

They had what they needed but not what they wanted. In light of this, let's reexamine this verse:

> So He humbled you, allowed you to hunger, and fed you
> with manna . . . that He might make you know that man
> shall not live by bread alone; but man lives by every word
> that proceeds from the mouth of the LORD. (Deuteronomy
> 8:3 NKJV)

God created hunger by removing anything that would have satisfied the desires and wants of their flesh, while still meeting their fundamental needs. And the hunger provided this test: God wanted them to see if they would desire Him instead of what they had left behind. Would they seek Him or what their flesh craved? Would they hunger and thirst for righteousness or for comfort and pleasure? Sadly, for the Israelites, their hearts weren't set on the only One who can satisfy, so they flunked the test:

> Then the foreign rabble who were traveling with the Israelites began to crave the good things of Egypt. And the people of Israel also began to complain. "Oh, for some meat!" they exclaimed. "We remember the fish we used to eat for

---

Survival Tips for Your Journey

#3 Resist Taking Matters into Your Own Hands

For those of us who are self-starting, get-'er-done Americans, one of the great temptations in the wilderness is to try to make something happen. When it feels like the Lord has left the building and is a million miles away, when even our modest attempts to do something for the kingdom fall flat, when hours in prayer only yield sore knees, in desperation we may do almost anything to make something happen. That's a bad idea. The wilderness is all about not much happening—a little water and a boring diet. In this barrenness, we learn that life is so much more than what we do or have. Instead, it's about who we know intimately and fulfilling His wishes each and every day.

In one of my wilderness stays, every day seemed

free in Egypt. And we had all the cucumbers, melons, leeks, onions, and garlic we wanted. But now our appetites are gone. All we ever see is this manna!" (Numbers 11:4–6)

They remembered what they had left behind in Egypt, where even a life in oppressive slavery now appeared preferable to the dry place where God had led them. They began to complain and murmur, crying out for meat. God heard their cry:

And He gave them their request, so they ate [meat—quail] and were well filled, for He gave them their own desire.

like a week to me, and every week seemed like a month because I had little vision, little passion, little drive. And yet I had to keep going. I had to push through, keep drawing from the Word of God in my heart, keep serving as best I could, keep showing up and refraining from doing something rash out of impatience. I had to continually remind myself that I was right where God wanted me. He was not wasting time and He would fulfill His promises.

And for certain, the wilderness is not the place to somehow try to promote yourself! Remember, you are being purified and prepared, so you must be diligent to stay steady and resist any temptation to sin.

On the highway in the wilderness that the Lord is building, always run well with Him. Don't ever decide to pass Him because it seems He is just moving too slow!

They were not deprived of their craving; But [He] sent leanness into their soul. (Psalms 106:15; 78:29–30 NKJV)

They got what they wanted, but at a high price. With this meat came leanness of the soul. This leanness made them unfit to endure, unable to pass the test and, ultimately, they never entered His Promised Land! The sin wasn't the request for meat, but rather, what that request represented. It revealed the dissatisfaction of their heart with God and His method of leading and providing. It also revealed their intense desire for the life left behind in Egypt, which they now remembered as pleasant, forgetting they had lived in slavery back there.

This is a sobering lesson for all of us: If we seek only the benefits of the promise and not the Promiser Himself, we will not have the strength needed for the desert moments of our life. Inevitably we will recall the good ol' days which, if viewed with a true perspective, were not good at all, but actually days of bondage.

It is one thing to seek the Lord for what He can *give you* or *do for you*. It is quite another to seek the Lord for *who He is*. The first option is for your benefit and your selfish motive will result, at best, in an immature relationship with God. But seeking the Lord for who and what He is will build the intimate and strong relationship we all desire.

Sanctified Scarcity

As we might expect, living in a barren wilderness involves scarcity of resources—a time when you get what you need emotionally, physically, or materially, rather than what you want. God has promised to take care of our basic needs, so in the wilderness He provides daily bread, not an abundance of things.

When times are good in America, we may say we are living high on the hog. In the wilderness there isn't even a single hog to be found! And the experience can involve different types of deprivation. It is a time when you experience what you need socially, not what you want. In the wilderness God knows what you need spiritually, and it may not be what you think you need! He meets our needs in this time—not necessarily our wants.

The purpose of the wilderness is to purify and strengthen us. Our pursuit is to be His *heart*, not His *provision*. Then when we come into abundant times, we won't forget that it is the Lord, our God, who gives us abundance in order to establish His covenant (Deuteronomy 8:2–18).

The fundamental problem is that *our* definition of needs and wants differs from reality. We call our wants "needs" when this is not so! Perhaps too many of us have yet to learn what Paul means:

> Not that I am implying that I was in any personal want,
> for I have learned how to be content (satisfied to the
> point where I am not disturbed or disquieted) in what-
> ever state I am. I know how to be abased and live hum-
> bly in straitened circumstances, and I know also how to
> enjoy plenty and live in abundance. I have learned in any
> and all circumstances the secret of facing every situation,
> whether well-fed or going hungry, having a sufficiency
> and enough to spare or going without and being in want.
> I have strength for all things in Christ Who empowers
> me. (Philippians 4:11–13 AMPC)

Paul learned through the strength of Christ that he could be as content in dry times as he was in abundance. We appear not to have learned contentment in the Western church either where, sadly, many with abundance are no more content than those who lack. If we do not possess all we feel is rightly ours, we think we are deprived. We judge men's faith and measure their spirituality by their possessions, how successful they are, or their social status when instead what we should value is their character and faith.

The children of Israel left Egypt with great possessions plundered from the Egyptians—articles of silver and gold and fine apparel. But they used the precious metals to build idols in the desert, then adorned themselves in fine apparel and danced before them. Clearly these possessions did not indicate godliness—in fact, the opposite was true. Only two of the original members of the exodus had the character to enter and possess the Promised Land. Only Joshua and Caleb entered, because they had a different spirit—they followed God fully (Numbers 14:24).

Our value system is warped if we measure one another by the standard of what we have and not who we are.

On the other hand, many times when a Christian comes into financial abundance, or perhaps into a position of leadership or influence, they view it as God's permission to do as they wish! They buy whatever they want, spending the money on their own desires, or use their position of influence to their benefit. Those who behave this way are most often those who mishandled the dry times. In actuality, financial blessing and greater authority should bring greater dependence on God for His purpose and leading.

Consider the attitude of Jesus in His ministry. He was not selfishly motivated. He took upon Himself our sin, sickness, and the death penalty. He valued our welfare as more important than His own, even though He was innocent of any sin. His purpose for life and ministry was not self-serving, but self-giving! Through denying Himself, He gave the greatest gift of all—eternal life.

Such maturity of character is developed in us by God when we are in the wilderness. The wilderness is where the fruit of the Spirit is cultivated. Watered by the intense desire to know Him, we learn to walk as He walks.

4

A RELATIONSHIP

It is astonishing, how many difficulties clear up without any effort when the inner life gets straightened out.

—A.W. Tozer

"If you love Me, you will obey My commandments."

—John 14:15 (NET)

W hat is God seeking for Himself when He arranges a wilderness trek for us? We've touched on some of our benefits and will continue to uncover more—but is there something in it for God as well? Yes, there is. He desires to strengthen the level of our relationship. He longs for us to be intimate with Him. Sadly, many of us seem prone to take advantage of our relationship with our Lord—allowing our passions to ebb.

When I was engaged to Lisa, I was head over heels in love with her. I thought of her constantly. I'd do whatever was necessary to spend as much time with her as possible. If she needed something, no matter what I was doing, I would jump in my car and get it for her.

I remember one time she and I spent close to five hours together at her parents' home. I reluctantly left. Almost as soon as I got to my place, my phone rang. It was Lisa and with a sweet, alluring voice she said, "Honey, you left your jacket at my house."

It was music to my ears. Without hesitation I excitedly responded, "Well then, I'll just have to come back over and pick it up."

I did and we spent another three to four hours together. It was a great day.

In those days if she would have called me in the middle of the night and said, "Honey, I'd love an ice cream cone," I would have happily responded, "I'll be there in the next ten minutes! What flavor do you want?" I would hunt for time and reasons to be with her. Because of my intense love for her, it was a joy for me to do whatever she wished. I didn't do these things to *prove* I loved her; I did them *because* I loved her.

I didn't have to force myself to talk to people about her . . . I sang her praises to anyone who would listen. If there was a lull in a conversation with someone, without any effort I would steer us to talk about Lisa and our upcoming marriage. I was in love!

Just a few short years into our marriage, though, I had turned my attention to other things, such as sports, activities with friends and, especially, the work of the ministry. It was now bothersome to spend quality time or do something for her. Lisa was not in my thoughts as much. Gifts for her came only on Christmas, anniversaries, and birthdays, and even that was a bit of a nuisance. In fact, one Valentine's Day I forgot to get her a present. She was heartbroken. I had no recourse but to apologize. The saddest reality was my immaturity to see the signs of our marriage season. Our union was strained; my first love was dying!

I'm so grateful that eventually God got my attention and turned my heart. He let me see how selfish I had become. Graciously, He rekindled the flames of our love and healed our marriage.

Something like this can occur in our relationship with God. Many followers of Christ reach a comfort zone or plateau where they begin to maintain rather than pursue. They're no longer chasing after God. They set their personal spiritual standards by comparing themselves to others or by what they feel is adequate. At this point, they stop seeking to know God deeply as a person.

Daily tasks, the pursuit of success, the cares of this life become the focus. Now God is sought for His blessings, rather than to know Him. They begin to err in their hearts, turning from God to self. They may continue to develop "Christian" friendships and build their status or position in the church, but they no longer yearn for the One who gives them life.

When we spend time seeking God's benefits and blessings, rather than desiring an intimate relationship with Him, we are easily misled. Let's be honest, we pat ourselves on the back for spending the time in prayer, but if we could see it from His vantage point, we'd realize we're attempting to use Him. He is reduced to a source of help in our time of need. But He loves us too much to leave us deceived. He will do for us what He did for these multitudes who were seeking Jesus:

> On the following day, when the people . . . saw that Jesus was not there, nor His disciples, they also got into boats and came to Capernaum, seeking Jesus. And when they found Him on the other side of the sea, they said to Him, "Rabbi, when did You come here?" Jesus answered them and said, "Most assuredly, I say to you, you seek Me, not because you saw the signs, but because you ate of the loaves and were filled." (John 6:22–26 NKJV)

Jesus knows the true motivation behind our actions. When the multitudes of people came *seeking Him*, He discerned that they were more interested in another blessing (free meal) than in seeing and understanding the signs. A sign gives direction or information—it doesn't point to itself. Jesus knew the crowds really weren't following Him because of the signs that revealed Who He is, but only so their stomachs would be filled.

Do you know a person who only contacts you when they need or want something from you? Or even worse, have you ever had someone seem to want to be your friend, only to find out later that they just wanted to get something—influence, money, material goods—from you? There was no genuine concern or love for you, but for a time you served their purpose. To be used like this is *painful*!

This selfish attitude has permeated society, as well as the body of Christ. Many in the church are discontented; their love for Jesus has chilled. They serve the Lord for personal benefit, not out of passionate love for who He is. So, as long as God provides for their *wants*, they are happy and excited about Him. But when trouble comes and life gets hard, the motive of their heart is revealed.

Any time the focus is *self*, complaining will be inevitable. Why? Because trouble or difficulty will eventually come. Once it does, the complaining, fueled by selfishness, will begin. As the difficulty continues, so will the complaining. This pattern is illustrated once again by the children of Israel. When the Lord delivered them from the horrors of life in Egypt under Pharaoh, the people rejoiced:

> Then Miriam the prophetess, the sister of Aaron, took the timbrel in her hand; and all the women went out after her with timbrels and with dances. And Miriam answered them: Sing to the LORD, for He has triumphed gloriously! The horse and its rider He has thrown into the sea! (Exodus 15:20–21 NKJV)

The people could not have been happier. They were overwhelmed by God's greatness, miraculous power, and goodness in delivering them from their captors. Yet only three days later, when they encountered the bitter waters in the wilderness of Shur, the complaining began: "What are we going to drink?" they asked Moses (Exodus 15:24). This didn't make much sense. Couldn't the same God who had just parted the Red Sea provide safe drinking water? Wasn't Moses the same heroic leader he'd been three days earlier?

God did, indeed, change the "bitter waters to sweet." But the memory of that miracle faded quickly too. A few days later, the people continued complaining—this time about the food. They murmured, "It was better for us before God delivered us." Really? Making bricks with guards beating your back with a whip is better?

> Then the whole congregation of the children of Israel complained against Moses and Aaron in the wilderness. And the children of Israel said to them, "Oh, that we had died by the hand of the LORD in Egypt, when we sat by the pots of meat and when we ate bread to the full!" (Exodus 16:2–3 NKJV)

In the hard, dry times when the complaining begins, it is usually directed at leaders, family members, friends, enemies—even the government. Most of us (out of fear) would never name God as the source of our troubles. So, likewise, the Israelites complained against Moses and Aaron, but no doubt what they were really thinking was, *It's the Lord who has let us down!* Moses saw through it and called them on the carpet: "'Your complaints *are* not against us but against the LORD'" (Exodus 16:8 NKJV).

The wilderness reveals the motives of our heart—whether

Survival Tips for Your Journey

#4 Clarify Your Agenda

During one of my early wilderness experiences, I was really struggling to keep my attitude positive because it seemed like nothing was ever going to change. In fact, it wasn't just the waiting that was bothering me—it was the pain I was experiencing during the wait. I was just tired of an annoying situation that seemed to be blocking me from moving into my God-given dream of a traveling/preaching ministry. The Lord had told me that He was using this wilderness to refine me. But one day, as once again I was pleading with the Lord for specifics as to why this "desert trek was taking so long," the Lord reminded me, "I want to see if you're serving Me or the dream."

Oh, man, did *that* get my attention! I had to put some more careful thought and prayer into determining if my true agenda was the very good dream of spreading the gospel all over the world—or the much better goal of obediently trusting God and waiting for Him to speak and move. Only then would I be in sync with His wishes.

So, my advice is: Don't let your wonderful God-given dream have a higher priority than living in God's presence and only doing what your Father desires.

they are *selfish* or *selfless*. Ask the Holy Spirit to show you what's really going on in your heart; what is driving you? What attitudes or behaviors are keeping you enslaved in your "Egypt" or causing you to complain in your wilderness? It's so vital to the health of your future to be honest and open to His loving correction.

The good news for each of us is that nothing is stopping us from repenting and changing the condition of our heart! In an instant we can stop the murmuring and begin seeking a relationship with God, instead of only using Him as a resource.

Out of love, then, God may send us to the wilderness.

God Is More than a Formula

God Himself was not the pursuit of the children of Israel, so they were unable to know His ways. They got excited about His mighty works, but whenever God's supernatural power was not on display, they strayed. If Moses was on the mountain, they drifted and played. They were satisfied with merely the benefits of salvation. There was no longing for more of God, and to know Him intimately.

One day in the wilderness, God told Moses to go down and tell the people to consecrate themselves, for He was coming to Mount Sinai to speak to them, just as earlier He had spoken to Moses. However, when the day came and the Lord showed up in magnificent splendor and display of His greatness, the people could not handle it:

All the people saw the thunderings, and the lightnings, and the noise of the trumpet, and the mountain smoking: and

when the people saw it, they removed, and stood afar off.
And they said unto Moses, "Speak thou with us, and we
will hear: but let not God speak with us, lest we die."
(Exodus 20:18–19 KJV)

They pleaded with Moses: "You talk to God for us and tell us what He says, and we will do it" (paraphrased), again showing their selfish desire for God's benefits without a *relationship* with Him. Maybe they had good intentions—they wanted to keep God's Word, but without an intimate *relationship* with Him they couldn't follow through.

The Israelites wanted answers to their problems instead of a relationship, so guess what—God gave them the Ten Commandments! But that didn't correct the problem either. With each generation that followed, the people proved they were unable to keep these commandments.

And what about our generation today? How many of us, with the best of intentions, try to keep the ways of God? We make vows and promises that we don't fulfill until we become so burdened that we can barely lift our voice in prayer. We may eventually turn to a pastor, our spouse, a friend, or a favorite blogger hoping that somehow we can appropriate their seeking of God as our own and improve our relationship with Him. Like the children of Israel, we try to keep God's Word—His commandments—without maintaining a life-giving, personal relationship with Him. Jesus says in John 14:21: "'Those who accept My commandments and obey them are the ones who love Me. And because they love Me, My Father will love them. And I will love them and reveal Myself to each of them.'"

I used to read that verse and think the Lord was saying, "John, if you keep My commandments, you will prove that you love Me." Then one day the Lord told me to read that verse again. When I did, He said, "You still aren't getting what I'm saying—read it again!" *Okay, Lord.* This went on until I'd read the verse nine or ten times.

Finally, I cried out, "Lord, forgive my ignorance; show me what You're saying!"

"John, I'm not saying that if you keep My commandments, you prove to Me that you love Me," He said. "I already know whether you love Me or not! What I'm saying is if a man falls head over heels in love with Me, he will be the one enabled to keep My commandments!"

I got it! It is *a relationship*, not *law*. I had viewed this as a command—law. What He revealed was the importance of a *relationship*.

- God can't be known through rules and regulations.
- God can't be found in methods.
- The Holy, Almighty One cannot be reduced to a formula!

Yet these are the perceptions many of us have of the Lord. In place of a relationship with God, we substitute "laws and formulas," like the seven steps to a happy life, the four-point plan of salvation, the five aspects of a successful relationship, the proven method to answered prayer. We imagine that God is somehow contained in a box of promises that can be pulled out, one at a time, and used as needed. If God is approached in this way, is it any wonder how hard sin is to deal with?

God is not the newest self-help formula! He's the Living God who inhabits His children—you and me. He wants to know us and be involved in all we are and do! This is about a heartfelt relationship. In light of this human proclivity to let our love diminish, you can understand why Jesus says:

"But I have this complaint against you. You don't love Me or each other as you did at first! Look how far you have fallen! Turn back to Me and do the works you did at first. If you don't repent, I will come and remove your lampstand from its place among the churches." (Revelation 2:4–5)

In contrast to the other Israelites, Moses was not content to worship God from afar. When he saw the appearance of God's presence, he didn't shrink back. He pressed in. Exodus 20:21 reads, "And the people stood afar off, and Moses drew near unto the thick darkness where God was" (KJV). Even though Moses was a man with influence and power, the leader of a nation of three million people, a man who had been part of the most astounding signs and wonders in the Old Testament, he knew these things alone would never satisfy him. Examine his prayer after he had experienced these amazing signs and wonders:

"Now therefore, I pray, if I have found grace in Your sight, show me now Your way, that I may know You and that I may find grace in Your sight . . . . If Your Presence does not go with us, do not bring us up from here. . . . Please, show me Your glory." (Exodus 33: 13–18 NKJV)

God had made Moses quite an offer. In the midst of the harsh wilderness, God told him to go and get the people and bring them to the Promised Land. He even offered to send a choice angel to make sure they got there safely. He reminded Moses how good the land would be—flowing with milk and honey, loaded with beautiful vistas, gardens, and orchards. But God said that He, personally, would not go with them. Once Moses heard this, he refused God's gracious offer. He in essence proclaimed, "I'd rather have Your presence without Your promises than the absence of Your presence with the promises." I'm sure God was delighted to be longed for like that.

Moses desired even more, so he boldly implored, "Show me now Your way, that I may know You" (Exodus 33:13 NKJV). In order to know God, we must know His *ways*! He reveals His ways to those seeking after His heart, not just His power or provision: But those who know His heart will walk in His power: "'. . . But the people that do know their God shall be strong, and do exploits'" (Daniel 11:32 KJV).

When I first entered the ministry, nearly every morning I spent one to two hours in prayer. My prayers went something like this: "God, use me to save souls, use me to heal the sick, use me to cast out devils." On and on I would pray—the same things in different words. I felt so selfless as I cried out to God for a far-reaching ministry.

Then one day, the Lord spoke to me and said, "Son, your prayers are selfish and off target." I was taken aback by what He'd said.

"What is your motive for wanting to do these things?" He asked. "All I hear from you is 'Use me to . . .'; *you* are the focus of the prayer. My purpose for creating you was not to have you win souls, cast out devils, or heal the sick. I created you for intimacy—that is your purpose."

This was startling to me. Then He showed me something I will never forget: *Judas got people free and healed the sick, all in Jesus's name!* Yes, when Jesus sent out the twelve, He sent all of them—including Judas, the one who later betrayed Him. My focus had been wrong. God's goal for us—His heavenly prize—is to *know Jesus Christ* (Philippians 3:10).

A few years later, Lisa was praying along the same lines as she prepared for a meeting. She and the Lord had a conversation. He said to her, "Lisa, I don't *use* people, I anoint them, I heal them, I transform them, I conform them to My image, but I don't *use* them." He continued by asking, "Lisa, have you ever been used by a friend?"

"Yes," she replied.

"How did you feel?" the Lord asked.

"I felt betrayed!"

The Lord went on: "Many ministers have cried for Me to only use them. 'Use me to heal, use me to influence, use me to save.' So I did, hoping all along for their heart, but they became too busy with the ministry for that. They never bothered to learn My ways, so they used the gift I gave them to build *their own* empire. When troubles hit, they cried out for Me but were offended when I did not answer their prayers in the time and manner they wished for. They felt used and became angry with Me. They fell away because they did not know Me."

What would you think of a woman whose only ambition was to produce children by her husband, with no interest in knowing him personally? She would fall at his feet and cry out, "Oh my husband, please *use me* to make babies for you! Please, please, give me babies or I will die!" It sounds absurd, yet it is not so different from us crying out to God for Him to "use us to get people saved," when we don't even have much of a relationship with Him ourselves. When we are intimate with God, children will be born—similar to what happens when a woman is intimate with her husband.

So the Israelites were not seeking and pursuing the right thing. They sought the *created* things, rather than the *Creator*. And we know what happened. Instead of the wilderness being a place of preparation—providing wisdom and strength for the challenges ahead—it became a land of futility, eventually claiming an entire generation. What a waste! The Promised Land was within reach.

What a lesson for all of us! The wilderness should be a welcomed time on this journey of glorious intimacy.

5

NEW WINE

"May we be vessels for Thy new Wine that renews all things."

—Ephrem the Syrian

"Do not remember the former things, Nor consider the things of old.

Behold, I will do a new thing, Now it shall spring forth; Shall you not know it? I will even make a road in the wilderness And rivers in the desert."

—Isaiah 43:18–19 (NKJV)

I n order to know God more intimately, we must welcome change. And there's no better locale than the wilderness to experience it. Here, in what may seem a most barren, forsaken place, we will witness a fresh move of His Spirit.

The question many wrestle with is: *Why does it take difficult or dry times to bring change?* Our discussion in this chapter will offer perspective.

Some time ago, after I had been through a difficult eighteen-month wilderness sojourn, I was chosen to lead a youth ministry (yes, it was quite a few years ago!). At the time, this church in Florida was one of the fastest growing in the United States, so I was a bit overwhelmed because I had no previous youth pastor experience. But I knew God had sent me, and if I diligently sought Him, all would be well.

This youth ministry was built on a traditional model of giving the kids a lot of cool activities. Sadly, many of these teenagers were not growing spiritually. Many were living loose lifestyles. So, when I took over, I sensed the Holy Spirit telling me, "Your message is to be on repentance, holiness, obedience, and lordship." So that's what I taught and preached, and in time the mood of the group changed dramatically.

The results were amazing. The youth group tripled in size within a matter of just months. Gang members, cult members, and young adults who were away from God were coming to know Jesus at a rapid rate. A lot of the backslidden youth of the previous group were catching fire. All of us were loving the rich presence of God and growing more in love with Him. God was blessing us and our efforts tremendously.

I assumed I was through with any kind of wilderness season since I had just come out of my first one in Dallas. I was now in my calling to preach the gospel. I figured since Jesus only went through one desert, it would be the same for me. How wrong I was. There was still a lot in store for me regarding purifying and strengthening, and more to learn about the desert season. And the wilderness I would eventually sojourn through next would make the previous eighteen months look like child's play.

The Holy Spirit was giving our leadership team so many innovative ideas. This is what happens when new wine from heaven is given, when we are "sent by God" after a season of desert preparation. He shows us how to be effective and fruitful, like Moses, David, Joseph, and others.

The growth we were experiencing with our youth was truly supernatural. Yet in the midst of all this success, I felt a strong burden for more than our local group. I felt we were to reach out to all the youth throughout central Florida. So, in prayer the idea arose, *What if we put the youth service on television?* Back then— the mid-1980s—that was the best way to reach people. There was no Internet, social media, YouTube, smartphones—nothing. I found out that one of the local, high-power TV stations had a potential viewing audience of four million people. Amazingly, this station had a 10 p.m. slot open on Saturday night. I knew this would be a good time to "catch" teenagers.

I ran the idea past our senior pastor, and he said we had no budget for this. So I asked him if I could challenge our young people to help raise money to fund a TV program. He gave us the go-ahead, so I presented a vision to the kids of how we could reach young people throughout central Florida who were strung out on drugs, alcohol, or facing other problems. The kids in the youth group caught the vision and with their earnings from newspaper routes, fast food jobs, retail positions, and other part-time employment, we raised enough money in pledges to go on that television station every Saturday night.

Our senior pastor was amazed and recognized that God was at work. This was the outcome of the new wine—who'd ever heard of a church youth group going on TV at 10 p.m. on Saturday night? But it worked. Soon we were seeing a rich harvest of souls who would not have heard the gospel if we'd not accepted the "new wine." For many years after leaving the youth pastor position, I heard testimonies of lives changed from the television program we called Youth Aflame.

Change Is Good

We'll get back to the youth group shortly. But first, let's identify what new wine is and why it's important.

Change that God nudges us toward is often not easy, but it's always good and fruitful. Often we resist change because it affects our comfort level. We certainly are creatures of habit. Once these patterns are established, it is uncomfortable to adjust them. But to be more effective in building His kingdom, we must be open to change.

If we were raised in a godly family, our faith practices, methods, and traditions were formed early and run deep. Not all traditions are wrong, of course, but when people respond merely from tradition and not from their heart, then faith expressions can be lifeless routines.

In fact, such routines can even become a religious stronghold. A person who has regressed to being religious is one who has an outward form of godliness, holding fast to what God *did*, while resisting what God is presently *doing*.

The Pharisees and other religious leaders of Jesus's day showed this type of behavior. They boasted that they were Abraham's children, sons of the covenant, and disciples of Moses. Holding fast to what God had done, they resisted the Son of God standing in their midst. They were zealous for their traditions and manner of worship, so they struggled when Jesus came, challenging every area of their comfort and stability. Jesus made it clear that God wasn't going to fit into their box . . . they would have to fit into His. They resisted this change and clung to their traditions.

One who is merely religious will breed an elitist attitude—"God will operate only through us and within our parameters"—which will result in prejudice and, eventually, hatred and betrayal if it is not checked. This is exactly what happened in Jesus's time and has happened throughout church history.

In order to change and make the transition from one level of faith and glory to the next, we must be willing to leave our comfort zone and pursue the way that God's Spirit leads us. This path will often take us through a wilderness where God causes new life to spring forth.

This pattern was apparent in the life of John the Baptist. His father was a priest—a high priest at one time. John's career path was to become a priest like his father. He was to go to school in Jerusalem and study to become a priest under the instruction of a famous teacher, Gamaliel. But one day the Spirit of the Lord began to call John to the wilderness. The more John prayed, the stronger was his inward urge to go to the wilderness. I'm sure a conflict arose within him and he may have had thoughts like these:

All my friends I've grown up with are going to "Bible school." They will get diplomas and be recognized as leaders.

They will be ordained and have the ability to preach in every synagogue in the country. What will they think of me? How will I ever fulfill my destiny if I don't go to "Bible School"?

I know there is a call on my life. My dad told me a high-ranking angel announced my birth and told him I would be a minister. But if I go out to this wilderness, nobody will ever know who I am. I'll never get invited to preach.

However, in his burning call to the wilderness, John overrode the questions bombarding his mind and decided to follow the Spirit to the desert. We read of him, "The child grew and became strong in spirit, and was in the deserts till the day of his manifestation to Israel" (Luke 1:80 NKJV). It's interesting to note that John started his desert training as a child and spent years of preparation for a ministry that was only six months long. Yet Jesus said he was the greatest prophet ever "born of a woman."

Scripture is silent about the length of time, the number of deserts, and the grueling circumstances John faced. Luke 3:2 reads,

"While Annas and Caiaphas were high priests, the Word of God came unto John the son of Zacharias in the wilderness" (NKJV). It's interesting to note that while Annas and Caiaphas were operating under what had become an out-of-sync religious system, a

---

Survival Tips for Your Journey

#5 Live in a Tent—Don't Build a House

Don't ever forget—the wilderness is temporary—you are just passing through. So while you are staying in the desert, live in a tent. And for sure, don't build a house!

Although the Israelites spent decades wandering in the wilderness, that was never God's plan. He didn't tell them to find the best situation possible and settle down—giving in to what seemed their reality by building houses. No, they lived in tents—always ready to pack up and move when the cloud began to move. The wilderness was always intended to be a temporary setting, not a destination. God never said, "Hey, this desert isn't so bad after all. Who needs a Promised Land? Let's start digging foundations and build proper houses—for you and Me." Yes, even God Himself lived in a tent during the entire wilderness trek.

Camping may be fun and even enjoyable for short periods of time, but most of us would rather leave the outdoors and live in a real house. Don't become disoriented and lay your foundation in the wilderness. Be ready at all times to pack up, move on, and eventually put your old tent in storage.

new vessel was being formed in the rough and dry places. This is where the new wine would be revealed.

God prepared John in the wilderness, not in the accepted "Bible school" of his day! Huge crowds of people from throughout Judea and Jerusalem came to hear the Word of the Lord spoken by John in the desert. A fresh move of the Spirit was beginning to blow—new wine was being released, but in the *desert*, not in the *religious places*. Those who were fed up with the religious hypocrisy and traditions went out to John with hearts willing to change in preparation for the appearing of God's Son.

Soon after this, Jesus came to be baptized by John in the Jordan River. Even though John felt unworthy to baptize Him, Jesus insisted on it. It was necessary for Jesus's ministry to come forth from what the Spirit of God was doing at that time on the earth. Jesus was then filled with the Spirit and immediately led into the wilderness.

The Bible is very clear that when Jesus was led into the wilderness, He was *filled* with the Spirit, but after the forty days of testing and temptation, He returned from the wilderness in the *power* of the Spirit. Now He was equipped for the ministry for which He'd come to earth. After only a few months of John the Baptist's ministry, another new thing had sprung forth from the wilderness—the ministry of Jesus Christ.

New Wineskins

Not long after Jesus began His ministry, we read, "One day some people said to Jesus, 'John the Baptist's disciples fast and pray regularly, and so do the disciples of the Pharisees. Why are your disciples always eating and and drinking?'" (Luke 5:33). The first question we must ask is "who are the 'some people'?" We find the answer in Matthew's Gospel: "One day the disciples of John the Baptist came to Jesus and asked . . ." (9:14). For years I thought it was the Pharisees, but the day I discovered it was the disciples of John the Baptist, it opened up this portion of Scripture in a totally new light! These men were annoyed because they often fasted from food and prayed long hours, but Jesus's disciples didn't operate this way. John's followers were doing all the sacrificing, yet Jesus's disciples were getting all the attention.

One of the ways the Spirit of God was moving in John's day was through much fasting. However, these disciples of John had not made the transition or change from the ministry pattern of John to what the Spirit of God was doing *now*. They believed their *method* of ministry and worship was what had brought the fruit. They had paid a great price to follow John the Baptist, leaving their families behind to live in the desert and eat insects, yet now their leader was in prison. This new Man had disciples with Him who were not playing by their rules. John's team was offended and in danger of developing a religious spirit.

Remember, religious spirits will always hold on to what God did, while resisting what He is *doing*. It is possible that John's followers had become more concerned about their loyalty to their leader and how his followers should behave than with what God was saying and doing *now*. Their focus was no longer the heart of God. The *method*, which at one time may have led to God's heart, was now their focus.

Pride and offense began to dominate. Those with John had invested time and, possibly, money into the ministry. Now all they had done, stood for, or obtained was threatened. So they dug in and resisted change, even though their leader had declared about Jesus, "He must become greater and greater, and I must become less and less" (John 3:30).

Look at how Jesus answers them: "'Do wedding guests fast while celebrating with the groom? Of course not'" (Luke 5:34). He exposes their religious ways by saying, "Why would they need to go on a fast when the Son of God is standing in their midst? All they need to do if they need something from God is come to Me" (paraphrased)! Religious thinking caused them to believe they had to earn God's favor through fasting and other religious activities. They saw fasting as a means of access to God, which they felt raised them above others who did not fast (or use their other methods). Thus, pride settled in. The method became more important than its original fruit.

Though there is benefit to fasting from food, it is not a way to manipulate God but instead to bring you into a position to better hear what God is saying. So why did the disciples need to fast to hear God's voice when He was right there with them? Look again at Luke 5:34–35: "Jesus responded, 'Do wedding guests fast while celebrating with the groom? Of course not. But someday the groom will be taken away from them, and then they will fast.'"

He does not say that they *might* fast in those days. He says they *will* fast. These men were talking about only fasting from food, but Jesus talks to them about a different fast. Notice this fast will be in the days that the Bridegroom is taken away. He is talking about a fast of His manifest presence, not only a fast from food. We know this because He goes on to explain it in the parable He is about to tell them. Remember that one of the definitions of the wilderness is the absence of the tangible presence of God.

Now look at the parable He gives to explain what He is saying:

"And no one puts new wine into old wineskins. For the new wine would burst the wineskins, spilling the wine and ruining the skins." (Luke 5:37)

In the Bible, wine is a symbol of God's presence. Paul says in Ephesians 5:18, "And do not be drunk with wine in which is dissipation; but be filled with the Spirit" (NKJV).

We are to be filled with wine, God's presence! New wine is a fresh move of His Spirit.

Let me briefly bring up this important question again. Do you remember how wonderful it was when you were first filled with the Spirit? God's presence was sweet and strong. Every time you would pray, His presence immediately would manifest itself, and you would sense His nearness all day long. At times in church you would just sit and cry because He was so close.

Then one day much later, you noticed that you didn't sense His presence quite so easily. You were still praying like you used to, but now you began to wonder, *God, where are You?!* You'd arrived at a wilderness!

There is a reason for that wilderness or fast of God's presence. God is preparing you to be a new wineskin. You can't put new wine, which is a fresh move of God's spirit, into old wineskins.

The wineskins used in Jesus's day were containers made of sheepskin. When the wine was first put in, the skins were flexible and pliable. They stretched easily and would yield without resistance as the wine expanded. However, as the years went by, the Middle Eastern atmosphere would dry out the wineskin, leaving it brittle and hard. Now if the wine was poured out and new wine poured in, the skin could handle neither the weight of the new wine nor any fermentation because it was rigid and brittle and would crack or tear easily. To correct this problem, the old wineskins would be soaked in water for several days and then rubbed with olive oil. That restored the wineskin's flexibility and pliableness.

This is symbolic of what happens to us, for we are the wineskin of the spiritual new wine. We are called to be carriers of God's presence. The atmosphere we reside in can draw out our tenderness to God's ways. We are not in heaven; we live in a corruptible environment called the world. Our minds therefore need to be renewed. To keep our wineskin pliable—ready always for the fresh wine—we must be soaked in the Word of God. Paul writes in Ephesians 5:26, "That He (Jesus) might sanctify and cleanse her (the church) with the washing of water by the Word" (NKJV). The rubbing of the wineskin with olive oil for us is like spending time seeking God in prayer. As we spend time with God, both in His Word and in prayer, our minds become renewed and we are no longer rigid in our ways and methods.

But in order to rejuvenate the old wineskin, you first have to pour out the old wine! That means no wine in the vessel—no tangible presence of God! That means a fast of the tangible presence of God, or as we have been saying continually, that means a dry time! In such a season you are preparing for *change*!

Why does God remove His tangible presence? To get you frustrated? No, even though that will occur! Is it because He wants to put you on the shelf until He has need of you? No! The reason He withdraws His presence is to cause you to seek and search for Him even more diligently. Seeking makes you flexible and pliable again. People who become rigid and inflexible are people who have stopped seeking God. They become set in their methods. They are set in the formulas that they themselves have devised from previous genuine experiences.

That was the condition of these men following John the Baptist. They attached to him because they could see the Lord was working mightily through him. However, instead of continuing to press on to the heavenly prize of knowing God intimately, they became rigid in their beliefs and methods.

In every move of God there is fresh teaching that comes forth. Teaching and sound doctrine are a means of bringing us to the heart of God. However, if we get stuck on our focus of the teaching or doctrine itself, then it will eventually bring us into religious bondage or legalism or error—or all of these.

You cannot know God through a rigid method of worship, and many Christians unknowingly succumb to this lifestyle. They establish their set patterns, steps, and routines of worship. Then, when they finally have the knowledge to be the model Christian, they stop *seeking* and settle down into the patterns or traditions they have developed. Yet, somehow they feel empty, even though, for them, they are living the complete gospel.

Jeremiah 29:12–13 says:

"'Then you will call upon Me and go and pray to Me, and
I will listen to you. And you will seek Me and find *Me,*
when you search for Me with all your heart.'" (NKJV)

Praying by itself is not enough to find Him. There are many who are bound by religious formulas who pray faithfully. God says that in your prayer there must be a diligent seeking of *Him.* He clearly states here that there will be searching, and that takes more than routine effort. It takes passionate desire and searching out His heart. That is why God says in Hebrews 11:6, "Anyone who wants to come to Him must believe that [He] exists and that He rewards those who sincerely seek Him."

Now let's look again at what Jesus says:

> "And no one puts new wine into old wineskins; or else the new wine will burst the wineskins and be spilled, and the wineskins will be ruined. But new wine must be put into new wineskins, and both are preserved. And no one, having drunk old wine, immediately desires new; for he says, 'The old is better.'" (Luke 5:37–39 NKJV)

No man who is used to the old wine will immediately desire the new wine. The key word here is "immediately," because we are human beings with habits and patterns. God must break those comfort zones by emptying the *old wine* and allowing us to go through a dry time of preparation with *no wine* in order that we might become thirsty for the *new wine.* When you are thirsty and there is nothing at all to drink, you won't complain, "I don't want this new wine, I want the old." If you are longing for the presence and power of God, you will be open to the fresh move of God's Spirit in your life. You will be like David, who said in his wilderness time:

> O God, You are my God;
> I earnestly search for You.

My soul thirsts for You;

> my whole body longs for You

in this parched and weary land

> where there is no water.

I have seen You in Your sanctuary

> and gazed upon Your power and glory. (Psalm 63:1–2)

David was thirsty for the power and presence of God. As a result, when he came into the work for which he was called, he was flexible to what the Lord desired—unlike King Saul who did things his own way and not God's way.

Another Wilderness Stay

As I related earlier in this chapter, my first real teaching ministry was as a youth pastor. The televised meetings were a great success. We also ran evangelistic radio spots on the second-most-popular secular station in our region. Everything was going great.

Then one day when I was praying, the Spirit of God told me that change was coming: "You will be removed from being youth pastor," He said, "and I will send you to churches and conferences in cities from the east coast to the west coast of America; from the Canadian border to the Mexican border; to Alaska and Hawaii . . . ."

I told Lisa what the Spirit had said, and the two of us pondered all this in our hearts, not sharing it with anyone else, except a pastor friend in a different state. God said He would do it, and I knew that if it was truly Him speaking, I wouldn't have to help God make it happen.

But nothing did happen for over a year. During that waiting period, getting into God's presence became harder and harder for me, until it seemed impossible. I was spending more time in prayer than ever before and still it seemed I was getting nowhere. Not only that, the original vision I'd had for the youth group seemed to be fading (the old wine was being poured out). The more I prayed, the more the vision dwindled. Nothing had changed outwardly, but inwardly my desire was declining.

I would spend hours in prayer before our youth services, and a couple of times I even begged God to get someone else to preach. I would go to the service feeling empty, but God's presence would fall on me like a blanket while I ministered. When I finished and was halfway home, though, His presence would lift for another week!

On top of it all, in the midst of all this, we went through internal and external trials like we had never experienced before. I wondered if there was something wrong with me, so I began to confess every sin I could recall that I might have committed, but there was no relief from my dryness.

One day after trying to figure out exactly what sin it was that I had committed, the Lord said to me, "You are not in this desert because you have sinned! I'm preparing you for the change that is coming."

He was developing within me the character I needed to handle the call of the coming phase of ministry. Look at Isaiah 43:18–19:

> "But forget all that—it is nothing compared to what I am
> going to do. For I am about to do something new. See, I
> have already begun! Do you not see it? I will make a path-

way through the wilderness. I will create rivers in the dry wasteland."

Later in this book, I will tell how in His timing the Lord miraculously revealed the specific details of "the change that was coming." All along, amid the most trying days of my wilderness, the Lord was preparing to birth our ministry to America and eventually the nations.

My friend, God will cause your *old* wine to dry up so that when the *new* comes, and the trials hit with the *new*, you won't desire to return to the *old*.

6

THE HEAVENLY PRIZE

Some people go back into the past and rake up all the troubles they ever had, and then they look into the future and anticipate that they will have still more trouble, and then they go reeling and staggering all through life.

—D.L. Moody

No, dear brothers and sisters, I have not achieved it, but I focus on this one thing: Forgetting the past and looking forward to what lies ahead, I press on to reach the end of the race and receive the heavenly prize for which God, through Christ Jesus, is calling us.

—Philippians 3:13–14

The Apostle Paul wrote two-thirds of the New Testament epistles and pioneered many of the gentile churches. His ministry spread to the whole world, and yet toward the end of his life, he said, *"I have not achieved it."* He wasn't satisfied—and he would not be until he reached the end of his race and received the heavenly prize.

In order for us to complete our race and receive our prize, the first thing we must settle in our hearts is that we haven't achieved or attained it as yet.

We are not perfected; we must continue to change and grow.

Moses, too, had a tremendous calling, led a nation of three million, and was part of miraculous signs and wonders like no one else in the Old Testament. However, God said that Moses was the meekest (most teachable) man on all the earth. He did not count himself to have arrived but continued to press on to finish his race and obtain the heavenly prize. In order to grow and change, we must be teachable.

The second thing we must do to finish our race for God is to *forget those things (victories and defeats) that are behind us!* Once again, here's what God says in Isaiah 43:18–19:

"But forget all that—
　　it is nothing compared to what I am going to do.
　　For I am about to do something new.
　　See, I have already begun! Do you not see it?
　I will make a pathway through the wilderness.
　　I will create rivers in the dry wasteland."

Past failures, rejections, or sins, if dwelled upon, will hinder us from moving forward in Christ. However, the *triumphs* of our past can hold us back as well. If we feel overconfident and sure of ourselves and begin to rely on past accomplishments to sustain and validate us, we will miss what God has for us now. This is exactly what God is saying in Isaiah 43. The former things were of Him, but in order to keep moving forward to accomplish what He intends for us, we must be ready to leave the ways God moved through us in the past. If we don't, we are in danger of becoming an old wineskin.

Paul also emphasizes this truth:

When I was a child, I spoke and thought and reasoned as a child. But when I grew up, I put away childish things. Now we see things imperfectly, like puzzling reflections in a mirror, but then we will see everything with perfect clarity. All that I know now is partial and incomplete, but then I will know everything completely, just as God now knows me completely. (1 Corinthians 13:11–12)

A child is not wrong; he is just immature. When I was five years old, my whole world seemed to be Tonka trucks and Legos.

A major accomplishment was saying the alphabet. I was seeing life through a dark glass, because I wasn't mature enough to handle the more complex and greater aspects of it.

When I was eighteen years old, Tonka trucks and Legos were a thing of the past. Now, after years of maturing, I was seeing life through a glass that was not quite so dark. My level and capacity for understanding had grown. When an eighteen-year-old acts like a five-year-old, it is abnormal. As we grow, we put away or

Survival Tips for Your Journey

#6 The "Not to Do" List

In the wilderness—based on what Scripture tells us about the regrettable experience of the Israelites—there are some things we must not do during our temporary stay in a dry place. In fact, this is a good list of what **not** to do at any time in the Christian life, but perhaps the temptation of these sins is greater when we are struggling in the desert. Here are the majors of, at least, a partial list:

1. Lust after evil things. When we are deprived, sometimes we think the wrong things will make us feel better, even happy.
2. Pursue idols. This is chasing our desires when we know that they are contrary to God's Word. Giving our love to someone or something above Jesus.
3. Give in to sexual temptation and immorality.
4. Tempt the Lord.
5. Complain, complain, complain.

forget former, childish ways and understandings, which are no longer useful or functional for our needs or enjoyment.

Likewise, while growing in the things of God, as we progress through life's stages, we should put away former, immature things. Paul was saying, now we see God's ways and His glory dimly, but as we pursue the heavenly prize, we will see clearer until we see God face to face. In other words, we will know Him as He knows us!

In his first letter to the believers at Corinth, Paul mentions that we can learn a great deal about how not to live from our wilderness ancestors:

> I don't want you to forget, dear brothers and sisters, about our ancestors in the wilderness long ago. . . . God was not pleased with most of them, and their bodies were scattered in the wilderness. These things happened as a warning to us, so that we would not crave evil things as they did. (1 Corinthians 10:1, 5–6)

The Israelites paid a great price, so let's learn from their example.

My friend, in the wilderness you can find God's ways and even His heart, but you have to be persistent and in your heart firmly say, "God, I believe You're good and that You love me, even when I don't feel Your goodness and love."

What is the heavenly prize Paul mentioned? He answered this in a previous verse. Philippians 3:10 says, "I want to know Christ and experience the mighty power that raised Him from the dead. I want to suffer with Him, sharing in His death." The heavenly prize of God is to be conformed into the image of His Son, Jesus Christ—to know Him as He knows us! Until we attain that goal, we should not be satisfied, so we must never cease to search for the heart of God.

The third thing we must do to pursue the heavenly prize is to "press toward the mark!" To press implies there will be resistance or pressure. There is opposition to knowing the Lord.

The greatest threat to the devil is a person conformed to the image of Jesus Christ, and the forces of darkness will fight that harder than anything. When believers are conformed to the image of Christ, they are no longer alive to themselves, but to the One who lives in them. They then enter into a more abundant, powerful expression of their life in Christ. That is why Paul said that in order to know Him, we must know the fellowship of His sufferings. The particular suffering of the flesh he speaks of coincides with the death of self, which will bring resurrection life! Peter writes:

> Therefore, since Christ suffered for us in the flesh, arm yourselves also with the same mind, for he who has suffered in the flesh has ceased from sin, that he no longer should live the rest *of his* time in the flesh for the lusts of men, but for the will of God. (1 Peter 4:1–2 NKJV)

If we have suffered in the flesh, we are no longer dominated or focused on our own way, pursuing all the sinful pursuits of the world. We have the character of Christ working in us! This is the goal we should be shooting for.

Suffering with Christ

What are the sufferings of Christ? Many have misunderstood this because certain religious teachings have perverted this biblical term. Suffering is *not* dying of disease or lacking the money to pay your bills. It is *not* going without food for weeks so that God will be moved by your sacrifice. Suffering is not sacrifice—it is obedience! The writer of Hebrews makes it clear what the sufferings of Christ are:

> While Jesus was here on earth, He offered prayers and pleadings, with a loud cry and tears, to the One who could rescue Him . . . . Even though Jesus was God's Son, He learned obedience from the things He suffered. (Hebrews 5:7–8)

Jesus didn't bring obedience to the earth; He had to learn it. He learned it by obeying His Father when it was easier to not obey. He didn't seek to please human beings, but God. He knew human beings would greatly benefit in the long run by His obedience. Peter identifies true suffering as living according to God's will as opposed to human desires (1 Peter 4:2).

The "sufferings of Christ" means going God's way when our mind, emotions, or physical senses are beckoning us to go the way of ease, compromise, or pleasure. This often occurs in the conflict we face when God tells *us* to go one way, but our friends, family, coworkers, or others desire us to go another way. Unfortunately, it

seems we usually encounter this resistance from the people clos-
est to us. A classic example of this is when Peter disagrees with
Jesus about His death and burial:

> From then on Jesus began to tell His disciples plainly that
> it was necessary for Him to go to Jerusalem, and that He
> would suffer many terrible things at the hands of the elders,
> the leading priests, and the teachers of religious law. He
> would be killed, but on the third day He would be raised
> from the dead. But Peter took Him aside and began to rep-
> rimand Him for saying such things. "Heaven forbid, Lord,"
> he said. "This will never happen to You!" Jesus turned
> to Peter and said, "Get away from Me, Satan! You are a
> dangerous trap to Me. You are seeing things merely from a
> human point of view, not from God's." (Matthew 16:21–23)

Jesus declared to His disciples that in order to obey God He
must go to Jerusalem, suffer, be killed, and be raised on the third
day. Peter obviously didn't hear the "resurrection part" of what
Jesus said, or he wouldn't have been so troubled by the statement
Jesus made about His coming death.

Can't you hear Peter's thoughts?

> *Wait a minute, You are the Messiah [it had just been*
> *revealed to him], and You are supposed to set up the*
> *kingdom and restore Israel. I have left my business, my*
> *wife, and family to follow You. I have lost friends to follow*
> *You. I have a lot of time invested in this. I've developed*
> *a reputation. The leaders of the synagogues think You*

*are crazy; the newspapers and magazines are constantly
writing articles about how controversial You are. You are
the hottest topic on social media, and most of the chatter
is unfavorable. You are considered by many established
theologians and leaders to be a heretic. And now You are
talking about death. Where will that leave me? All this
time invested in following You, and I'll be left with nothing
but a bad reputation.*

Then Peter blurted out, "No, Lord, You can't do this!"
(paraphrased).

Jesus had to point out quickly that Peter's thoughts were selfish and worldly. He was not seeing things through God's eyes. The
world is trained by Satan ("the god of this world" 2 Corinthians
4:4) to look out for its own interests. The kingdom of heaven is
just the opposite. So in order to fulfill the will of God, we must
go against the flow of culture, even if that means we have to go
against a "brother or sister in the Lord" whose thinking is too
influenced by the world. Peter was not a wicked man, but his
thought process in this matter was conformed to the world, not to
Christ. He was resisting a change in his perspective of how things
should be or turn out.

Another example of this is the children of Israel spying out
the land of Canaan. They had been in the wilderness for over a
year when God told Moses to send men to gather intelligence on
the Promised Land, which He wanted them to have. Moses chose
twelve leaders, one from each tribe. Two of them were Joshua and
Caleb.

When the intelligence operatives returned from spying out

the land, they gave conflicting reports of what they'd seen and what action should be taken. Ten of the men said:

> "The people living there are powerful, and their towns are large and fortified. We even saw giants there, the descendants of Anak! The Amalekites live in the Negev, and the Hittites, Jebusites, and Amorites live in the hill country. The Canaanites live along the coast of the Mediterranean Sea and along the Jordan Valley. . . . We can't go up against them! They are stronger than we are!" So they spread this bad report about the land among the Israelites: "The land we traveled through and explored will devour anyone who goes to live there. All the people we saw were huge." (Numbers 13:28–29, 31–32)

Caleb and Joshua brought back a different report:

> But Caleb tried to quiet the people as they stood before Moses. "Let's go at once to take the land," he said. "We can certainly conquer it! . . . And if the LORD is pleased with us, he will bring us safely into that land and give it to us. It is a rich land flowing with milk and honey. Do not rebel against the LORD, and don't be afraid of the people of the land. They are only helpless prey to us! They have no protection, but the LORD is with us! Don't be afraid of them!" (Numbers 13:30; 14:8–9)

All twelve had traveled together to spy on the land. They had seen the same land, cities, and people. Why did ten come back reporting on it one way and two return with just the opposite report? Perspective!

God said about Caleb and Joshua that they had a different spirit because they followed Him fully (Numbers 14:24). In other words, they had moved away from men's desires to God's will. They saw through God's eyes, not through the perspective of self-preservation. This is the key to understanding why ten spies saw the same things differently than Joshua and Caleb. The ten were more concerned about their comfort, security, and families than God's desires. Their lives were led by what would affect them, not the kingdom of God. They failed in knowing that God would never abandon them and would give success in whatever He put before them. This wrong thinking was true of the rest of the population as well, for they said:

> Their voices rose in a great chorus of protest against Moses
> and Aaron. "If only we had died in Egypt, or even here in
> the wilderness!" they complained. "Why is the LORD taking
> us to this country only to have us die in battle? Our wives
> and our little ones will be carried off as plunder! Wouldn't
> it be better for us to return to Egypt?" (Numbers 14:2–3)

The children of Israel were looking back to the "good ol' days" of Egypt, when their bellies were filled and there was some stability. Even though they had been slaves in Egypt, what they were facing now looked much more difficult than even their bondage. All of them were resisting a necessary change. They found security in the familiarity of the desert, even though their nomadic lifestyle and dietary choices were less than ideal. As a result, they never saw the Promised Land and never fulfilled the will of God for their lives.

Joshua and Caleb, however, had to *press* on. The resistance they had to face came from their own "brothers" who wanted to totally silence them: "But the whole community began to talk about stoning Joshua and Caleb" (Numbers 14:10). Those who opposed Joshua and Caleb had unrenewed minds and were still conformed to think and see things as the world does. And they were stuck in their ways . . . and stuck in desert thinking.

Like Joshua and Caleb before him, the apostle Paul said that he had to forget those things that were behind and *press* on toward the heavenly prize (Philippians 3:14).

Look again at Isaiah 43:18–19, some instruction that certainly should encourage us today:

> "But forget all that—
>   it is nothing compared to what I am going to do.
> For I am about to do something new.
>   See, I have already begun! Do you not see it?
> I will make a pathway through the wilderness.
>   I will create rivers in the dry wasteland."

Sadly, even today there are many who would rather stay in the "security" of their bondage than press into freedom, fulfilling the will of God for them. They fear the change ahead more than their familiar but oppressive surroundings. There are others who are satisfied with what God has done in the past and are unwilling to press on to new challenges. God has indeed done great things *how do we do this?*

through them, but they've camped on the plateau of their previous successes.

Obeying the will of God brings life and liberty and is the only way to find true fulfillment. However, pressing on to the heavenly prize may look impossible in your current circumstances. Through Isaiah, God said He would do a new thing, but it would "spring forth in the wilderness." In other words, as we follow the Spirit of God to accomplish what He desires, we will find ourselves in what appears to be an impossible, dry situation. But as we know, what seems impossible to men is possible to God (Luke 18:27). For on the other side of your current wilderness are abundant life, conquest, and fulfillment.

Don't be like the ten spies and all the others who were unwilling to embrace God's desires and resisted the change that would have released them from the deprivations of the wilderness. Instead, with confidence, strike out for the promised land of God's heavenly prize for you!

7

GOD'S SUPER HIGHWAY

Adversity is not simply a tool. It is God's most effective tool for the advancement of our spiritual lives. The circumstances and events that we see as setbacks are oftentimes the very things that launch us into periods of intense spiritual growth. Once we begin to understand this, and accept it as a spiritual fact of life, adversity becomes easier to bear.

—Charles Stanley

*Listen! It's the voice of someone shouting,
"Clear the way through the wilderness
      for the LORD!
Make a straight highway through the wasteland
      for our God!"*

—Isaiah 40:3

Surprising as it may seem, the wilderness is where God has located a super highway! This is where His way is prepared, the road to the high or exalted life of how God lives and thinks.

In all of history, few have followed this highway. Yet now, God is preparing many to journey upon it. We find this described in Isaiah 35:6, 8:

> For waters shall burst forth in the wilderness, and streams
> in the desert . . . . A highway shall be there, and a road, and
> it shall be called the Highway of Holiness. (NKJV)

God's highway in the wilderness does not have an iconic number like I-95 or Route 66. It is simply called *holiness*.

One of the definitions of holiness is "the state of being pure." Jesus says, "God blesses those whose hearts are pure, for they will see God" (Matthew 5:8). Jesus will not return for an unholy or impure church; He is coming for a church without a spot or wrinkle.

Several decades ago, when I was still a young man just beginning in ministry, the Lord showed me while praying one day that He was going to begin purifying my life. I got so excited, I told

Lisa, "God is going to remove my impurities," and I proceeded to tell her all the undesirable things God would be removing. (She may have even added a few I had left off the list!)

Then, for the next three months, nothing happened. As a matter of fact, things worsened in my life, and I found myself more in need of purification. I went to the Lord and asked, "Why are my bad habits getting worse, not better?"

"Son," He responded. "I said that *I* was going to purify you. You have been trying to do it in your own strength. Now I will do it *My* way." I had no idea that I was about to move into my first wilderness journey and that it would last eighteen months.

His Ways Are Not Our Ways

Early in my life as a believer, I became acquainted with the ministry of T.L. Osborn. Dr. Osborn was a tremendous minister and author who, along with his wife, Daisy, had a powerful evangelistic and miraculous healing ministry for several decades throughout the world. Their ministry led tens of millions to salvation.

So you can imagine how excited I was to meet Dr. Osborn when he came to Dallas to preach at our church. On top of it, because of my job as a host for the guest speakers, I got to know him personally. T.L. was amazing. When I was with him, I felt like I was sitting with Jesus.

T.L. came to our church several times and we became very close. He gave me all the books he'd studied as a young man preparing for ministry. He also gave me many of his clothes (we were the exact same size) on two separate occasions. Lisa and I had no budget for dress clothes in those days, so I got a lot of use out of those two wardrobes. After these visits, he and Daisy became like a father and mother to Lisa and me.

Years earlier, when I still worked in corporate America, in a service one day when T.L. was preaching, the Holy Spirit whispered to me, *Someday you'll serve him. You'll work for Dr. Osborn.* So, in my mind, I thought this confirmed that I would be on his team, and in the future I would start a similar evangelistic ministry.

But in the meantime, nothing happened—I was still in the wilderness. The Osborns had their ministry headquarters in Tulsa, but they lived in Orlando. As time went on, I felt so much internal pressure to get on with my ministry that I decided I needed to move to Orlando so I could get closer to the Osborns. My thoughts were twofold. First, it would make it apparent to T.L. that I was no longer serving at a church. He was a man of impeccable integrity. I knew he would never hire me away from our church. Second, since Lisa and I would be living in Orlando, it would be easy to join them in ministry. I would make myself accessible to him once we moved to Florida.

This was all a bit over the top—I know. But I was so eager to "help" God get me headed into my true calling.

So, I made an appointment with my pastor in Dallas to let him know I was resigning and moving to Orlando. Then, the night before my appointment, three pastors from three different cities called me. Each of them, upon learning what I was going to do the next day, asked the exact same question, "Is Lisa in full agreement with you?"

She wasn't. A few times she'd said to me, "John, I will submit to your direction, but I can't tell you I feel in my heart that this is the right thing to do." I shrugged her comments off. I thought, *Lisa just doesn't see it, and since I'm the head of the home, she needs to submit to my direction.* Oh, how immature and stupid my thoughts were.

When I got the call from the third pastor late that night, and when he asked the same question as the previous two, something broke in me. My eyes were opened, and I could see that I was trying to help God bring to pass His plan instead of letting Him do it.

The next day, Lisa and I met with my pastor and his wife. I told them both why I had asked for the meeting but that after the three calls the night before, I had changed my mind. They both were very gracious and informed Lisa and me that they still wanted us to stay on with them. My place and position were still available.

I felt like a load of weight came off my shoulders, and I was now ready to see God work on our behalf. I had no idea my purging process was not yet finished. There was another wave to come, and it would begin that very day.

Just six hours after the meeting with our pastor and his wife, I was at home changing into my gym clothes to go play pickup basketball with fellow employees of our church. The phone rang. It was T.L. Osborn! To say the least, I was in shock.

During that ninety-minute phone call, he offered both Lisa and me positions in their ministry. We were going to assist Daisy and him, and travel with them all over the world. We would also pioneer a church in Tulsa that eventually would become a prototype for other church plants. The goal would then be to start similar churches in the places around the world where they held their massive crusades.

I repeatedly thought during the long phone call, *Wow, Father, I knew You would act, but I'm amazed at how quickly You did!* It's hard to articulate both the shock and excitement I was experiencing while on the phone with T.L. I was sure this was the exit from the wilderness I'd been waiting for. I was so happy I felt like I could jump and hit the ceiling of my apartment with my head. After hanging up the phone, I walked outside to thank God, but I felt a check or hesitation in my spirit. It was like an uncomfortable, gnawing feeling deep inside.

I thought, *No, God, no, no, no, You can't do this! This is something You promised me long ago, that one day I would work for T.L. Osborn! You can't say no to this!*

The check wouldn't leave. I tried as hard as I could for three days to cause it to leave in prayer, trying to rid myself of the uneasy feeling. "God, give me joy about this!" I cried out. Lisa felt the check too, even though she really wanted to work with the Osborns as well.

In the end, I absolutely chose to not believe this hesitation could be from God (another immature and even dangerous move on my part). So Lisa and I flew to Oklahoma for an interview, and everything appeared to be coming together. T.L. and Daisy officially offered us the positions and introduced us to their entire team at their Christmas party.

We came back to Dallas and I resigned from my position at the church. But the check did not go away. I was spending hours in prayer and was still uneasy. I kept trying to force the uncomfortable feeling away by praying longer. Nothing was changing.

Finally, I said to Lisa, "I don't know what's going on, but something just is not right." She agreed, "Something is not right with me, either."

I called T.L. and told him how I felt. He said, "You know, let's all get together and talk about this." So we flew to Tulsa and after meeting for two hours, T.L. said, "We offered you this position because we really love you and we know you love us. But we're beginning to think that maybe this isn't God."

"I don't understand it either," I said, "but I think you're right." I could hardly believe what was coming out of my mouth. It took everything in me to say that. That was the dream of my life, to work for T.L. Osborn.

In those years, it was my practice to go out early in the morning and pray for an hour and a half to two hours. But after this disappointment related to my hero, Dr. Osborn, for at least two weeks, I barely prayed when I went out early in the morning. It seemed all I could do was cry. All I could do was go over what had happened in the past few months in disbelief. The sorrow was indescribable. It was as if I was mourning the death of a loved one. After two weeks of this, I was outside where nobody could hear me, so I just screamed at the top of my voice, "*Why?!* Why did You have me give this up? Six years ago, You spoke to me and said I'd work for him. *Why?!*"

I'll never forget what the Lord said to me: "Because I wanted to see if you were serving Me or the dream."

I was stunned.

Then He said, "That's why I had Abraham put Isaac on the altar, because I wanted to see if his love for Me was less than the promised blessing I gave him. It would prove if he was serving the dream, serving Me to get the dream, or if he was serving Me and trusting My integrity for the fulfillment of the dream."

It was as if every question I had wrestled with over the past couple of weeks was answered with His statement. And for the first time in over eighteen months, I had an explosion of joy in my spirit. It was as if my life reopened and I recognized how blessed I was in that moment. I realized I was married to a beautiful lady. I realized we had an amazing young baby. I fell in love with my wife again, along with my son. I realized that we lived in a brand-new apartment that was only thirty steps from a beautiful pool, and we had bright sunny skies most days. I had lost sight of all of that, because I was so consumed with the pressure of ministry—what I thought I had to be doing to please God.

Looking back now, I realize when God said that I was going

Survival Tips for Your Journey

#7 Choose Your Friends Carefully

Maybe it shouldn't surprise us, but often our most hurtful critics and opponents are people we thought were on our team! Often persecution comes from someone you thought was your friend.

The wilderness may involve actual persecution, and we need to be aware that persecution is to be expected if we follow Christ. The apostle Paul says, "Yes, and everyone who wants to live a godly life in Christ Jesus will suffer persecution" (2 Timothy 3:12). The persecution is part of the refining process. And who might do the persecuting? For one, the impostors—the ones who have infiltrated God's people, appearing as believers when they really don't have a heart for God. That is why Paul speaks of Jannes and Jambres resisting Moses. These were people in the congregation of the Lord, not outsiders.

to work for T.L. Osborn, I had already had that privilege, serving him many, many times when he came to our church in Dallas.

But now I had no job. I went back to the church, hat in hand, to find out if I could have my job back. I remember looking at my friend, who was one of the associate pastors, and saying, "I feel so small I think I could walk underneath that door"—those were my exact words. I had told everybody I would be working for T.L. and Daisy. Our pastor even announced it from the platform—and now that wasn't happening.

Paul describes some of the persecutions and perils he faced, and he tells us that some of the afflictions he encountered were from "false brethren" (2 Corinthians 11:26 NKJV).

In the wilderness it helps to have people who love and care for you; people who will speak God's will into your life. You don't need critics and those who encourage you to disobey God, such as Job's wife and his friends did. And you don't need false prophets who flatter you when you need godly correction. You need those who love you and speak God's wisdom to you.

But be alert: If anyone begins to criticize you and even blame you for being the cause of your wilderness, that person may not truly be a friend. The Holy Spirit will convict us of sin, and often He will use someone else to help us see our error and repent. But ongoing accusations that offer no hope are motivated by the enemy. Beware!

The church graciously gave me a part-time job. I served there for eight more months. Then, what God had prepared me for—the next phase of His calling—occurred. I was asked to come be a team member at one of the fastest-growing churches in America. I would be their youth pastor. It happened miraculously. Lisa and I both knew this was God's door. I now had new life and a fresh vision because I was now a prepared wineskin for this new position that would carry the fresh new wine.

The Purification Path

For centuries, actually since Jesus left the earth, His followers have been trying to achieve holiness through their own ability. In fact, whole church denominations have been birthed as a result of futile attempts to be pure. But all we have done is enslave ourselves to the bondage of legalism, because holiness is a work of God's grace, not an outward restriction of the flesh.

God gives grace to the humble, not the proud. The proud person thinks holiness can be achieved without God's help by following written guidelines, rules, and regulations. The humble person knows this is futile and relies on the grace (strength) of the Lord. A close relationship with God is pure, because only through such a relationship can anyone be empowered to keep the laws written on the heart.

Many of us have tried to attain holiness by obeying the letter of the New Testament or unscriptural convictions, and have failed miserably. Like the Jews who tried unsuccessfully to receive salvation by keeping the letter of the law, so even are we unable to walk in holiness by keeping these rules. Many have restricted themselves with legalistic ideas about certain behaviors or activities. All these outward limits are established in an attempt to obtain inward purity.

But God is not looking for an outward form of holiness; He wants an inward change of your heart, for a pure heart will produce pure conduct. Jesus said in Matthew 23:26, "First cleanse the inside of the cup and dish [the heart], that the outside of them may be clean also" (NKJV).

If your heart is pure, you will not desire to act in a way that dishonors Jesus. You will stay away from those porn sites on the Internet or you won't wear provocative clothing. A man or woman can boast that they have never been divorced, yet lust in their heart for someone down the hall at the office, or periodically view porn sites on the web. Is this holiness?

If your heart is pure, a computer or smartphone will not cause you to search out unedifying material. The technology itself is not what makes you impure. It's what is in your heart that makes that determination. If your heart is pure, you will desire only what God desires.

The wilderness is one of the crucibles God uses to purify our motives and intentions. God is in the process of preparing our hearts prior to His return for His church. God is raising a generation of people that will show *His* glory, not their own—a people made in His image, walking in His character:

> But in a great house there are not only vessels of gold and silver, but also of wood and clay, some for honor and some for dishonor. Therefore if anyone cleanses himself from the latter (sin/iniquity), he will be a vessel for honor, sanctified

and useful for the Master, prepared for every good work.
(2 Timothy 2:20–21 NKJV)

Notice that there are two types of vessels—honorable and dishonorable. The Greek word for dishonor, *atimia*, is defined as "dishonor, reproach, shame, vile." The Greek word for honor is *time*, which is defined as "precious." God says, "If you take out the precious from the vile, you shall be as My mouth" (Jeremiah 15:19 NKJV). The precious is taken from the vile through a thorough cleansing or freeing from impurities.

Malachi is an Old Testament prophet who prophesied heavily about New Testament times. The problem he faced is that he didn't have New Testament terminology. So, he used terms such as "Levites" and "priests" to identify what he was seeing and being told about New Testament Christians by the Holy Spirit.

Malachi foretold that the Lord would come *to* His temple (His church), before coming *for* His temple. The purpose: to purify. He writes:

He will sit like a refiner of silver, burning away the dross. He will purify the Levites, refining them like gold and silver, so that they may once again offer acceptable sacrifices to the Lord (Malachi 3:3).

The Levites are a foreshadowing of "the royal priests" (1 Peter 2:9), which are Christ followers in the church. Since God compares the refinement of this priesthood to the refinement process for gold and silver, it is helpful to understand the characteristics of gold and silver and how they are refined. I will discuss only gold, since the refining process is similar for both metals.

Gold has a beautiful yellow color, emitting a soft metallic glow. It is widely found in nature but always in small quantities and rarely in a pure state. When purified, gold is soft, pliable, and free from corrosion or other substances. If gold is mixed with other metals (copper, iron, nickel), it becomes harder, less pliable, and more corrosive. This mixture is called an alloy. The higher the percentage of another metal, the harder the gold becomes. Conversely, the lower the percentage of alloy, the softer and more flexible it is.

Immediately we see the parallel: A pure heart before God is like pure gold. A pure heart is soft, tender, and pliable; Therefore, as the Holy Spirit says:

> "Today when you hear His voice,
>   don't harden your hearts
> as Israel did when they rebelled,
>   when they tested Me in the wilderness. . . ."
> You must warn each other every day, while it is still "today,"
> so that none of you will be deceived by sin and hardened. . . .
> (Hebrews 3:7–8, 13)

Sin is the added substance that turns our *pure* gold into an alloy, hardening our hearts. This lack of tenderness creates a loss of sensitivity, which hinders our ability to hear the Lord's voice.

Unfortunately, today this is the state of too many who have a form of godliness, but not a tender heart that burns for Jesus. That white-hot love for God has been replaced with a frigid self-love, which seeks only its own pleasure, comfort, and benefit. Supposing that godliness is a means to personal gain (1 Timothy 6:5), they seek only the benefits of the promises and unknowingly or conveniently exclude the Promiser Himself. In a state of deception, they delight themselves with the things of the world, expecting to receive heaven too! This is not what God desires:

> Pure and genuine religion in the sight of God the Father means . . . refusing to let the world corrupt you. (James 1:27)

Jesus is going to come back for a church that is holy, without spot, blemish, or any such impurity (Ephesians 5:27), a body of people whose hearts are unpolluted by the world's ways.

Another characteristic of gold is its resistance to rust or corrosion. Even though other metals tarnish from atmospheric conditions, this does not affect pure gold in the same way. Brass (a yellow alloy of copper and zinc), though it resembles gold, does not behave as gold. Brass tarnishes easily. It has gold's appearance without possessing its character. In the church we have brass vessels, those who have the appearance of gold, but they are not. Only the refining fire will show the difference between the two. Malachi says after the refining:

> "Then you will again see the difference between the righteous and the wicked, between those who serve God and those who do not." (Malachi 3:18)

Let's return to discussing the refining of gold. A higher percentage of foreign substances in gold makes it not only harder but more susceptible to corrosion and corruption. It is more easily influenced by the atmosphere of the world we live in.

Presently, the world's ways have leaked into the church. We have become infiltrated by its culture, and thus we are tarnished. In America, the church's values are polluted with worldliness. Many are insensitive and do not realize the need for purification.

Malachi 3:3 shows how Jesus will refine (or purge) His church from the influence of the world, just as a refiner purifies gold. In the refining process, gold is ground into powder and then mixed with a substance called flux. The two are then placed in a furnace and melted by an intense fire. The alloys or impurities are drawn to the flux and rise to the surface. The gold (which is heavier) remains at the bottom. The impurities or dross (such as copper, iron, and zinc, combined with flux) are then removed.

Now look closely at how God refines:

I will turn My hand against you, and thoroughly purge away your dross, and take away all your alloy. I will restore your judges [leaders] as at the first, and your counselors [believers] as at the beginning. Afterward you shall be called the city of righteousness, the faithful city. (Isaiah 1:25–26 NKJV)

What is the fire God uses for refining us? The answer is found in the following passage:

In this you greatly rejoice, though now for a little while, if need be, you have been grieved [distressed] by various trials, that the genuineness of your faith, being much more precious than gold that perishes, though it [your faith] is tested by fire, may be found to praise, honor, and glory at the revelation of Jesus Christ. (1 Peter 1:6–7 NKJV)

God's fire for refining is *trials* and *tribulations*, which of course is the central theme of the wilderness. The heat of these separates our impurities from the character of God in our lives. This potentially leads to holiness (I will explain shortly why I say "potentially").

Another characteristic of gold in its purest state is its transparency (defined as the ability to see through, as glass). "And the street of the city [was] pure gold, like transparent glass" (Revelation 21:21 NKJV). Once you are purified by the fiery trials, you become transparent! A transparent vessel brings no glory to itself, but it glorifies what it contains. It is unobstructive and almost unnoticeable.

Once we are refined, the world again will see Jesus. If we are transparent—people who tell the truth, do not put on airs, keep our word, have integrity, live with nothing to hide—the people of the world will notice.

In Isaiah, this is amplified to a greater degree:

I have refined you, but not as silver is refined. Rather, I have refined you in the furnace of suffering. I will rescue you for My sake—yes, for My own sake! I will not let My reputation be tarnished, and I will not share My glory with idols! (Isaiah 48:10–11)

The fire or furnace is affliction, not a literal physical fire, as with which silver (or gold) is refined, which explains why He says, *"but not as silver."* Our trials are the intense heat that separates the precious from the vile.

God does not remove them against our will. That is why Paul says in 2 Timothy 2:21, that the person wanting to be purified "cleanses himself." If you want to justify or make excuses and continue to allow flaws to hold you back, God will not force you to release them. The process of suffering will have no value (which is why I wrote "potentially" earlier). Purification on the highway of holiness is a constant, ongoing, and often painful process. However, knowing its yield, I welcome it.

The writer of Hebrews states, "Pursue . . . holiness, without which no one will see the Lord" (12:14 NKJV). Jesus says, "Blessed are the pure in heart, for they shall see God" (Matthew 5:8 NKJV). David, who had a heart after God, cried out, "How can I know all the sins lurking in my heart? Cleanse me from these hidden faults" (Psalm 19:12).

Let this be our cry. If we ask God to purify our hearts, He will remove those impurities hidden from our eyes. God knows our innermost thoughts and intents, even though we don't.

I urge you to learn how to recognize and welcome the spiritual time and season of the wilderness. As fiery trials hit, don't become angry and blame others, but look for their purpose. Examine your heart and allow God to remove the vile from the precious. He commands, "'You must be holy because I am holy'" (1 Peter 1:16).

Remember, refinement strengthens that which is already good and cleanses or removes that which weakens or defiles. Welcome His refining so that you might be a vessel of honor, able to beautifully and transparently show His glory.

8

BUILD WELL

No stars gleam as brightly as those which glisten in the polar sky. No water tastes so sweet as that which springs amid the desert sand. And no faith is so precious as that which lives and triumphs through adversity. Tested faith brings experience. You would never have believed your own weakness had you not needed to pass through trials. And you would never have known God's strength had His strength not been needed to carry you through.

—Charles H. Spurgeon

For those who live according to the flesh set their minds on the things of the flesh, but those who live according to the Spirit, the things of the Spirit.

—Romans 8:5 (NKJV)

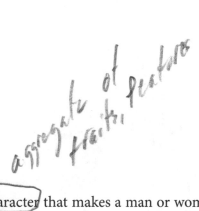

It is character that makes a man or woman of God, not anointing. And it's in the wilderness, when the pressure comes, when the disappointments mount, when the dreams seem to be unattainable, that necessary refining—character shaping—takes place.

I recall a time in the wilderness when I was struggling to overcome a lot of anger. I shared this in the first chapter. So I asked God, "Why am I so angry at everyone? What do I need to bind or cast out of my life?"

He responded, "Son, you can't bind or cast out flesh, you crucify it."

Now, even more frustrated, I asked, "Well then, where is this anger coming from? I've never experienced this before, not even before I was saved!"

"It's been in you for years," He answered, "but it's invisible, just as the impurities in your gold ring—before it's melted in the furnace—are invisible. But when you put it in the furnace, the impurities come to the surface. Now I've made your anger visible to you by bringing you into this furnace of affliction."

I wasn't quite sure what to make of what God was saying to me. So He added more detail: "You can blame your wife, blame your co-workers, blame your friends, blame the pressure of having a newborn child, blame your circumstances. If you do, the anger will remain and when the heat lessens, it will go right back down in you, and the process will need to start all over again. Or you can repent by praying, 'God, I'm so sorry, take this anger out of me.' If you do this, then I'll take My big ladle and scoop it right out of you."

So that's what I did. As the pressure of the fiery wilderness exposed my anger, I confessed my sin, repented, and asked Him to take it away.

This is one reason the wilderness—as tough as it can be—is so valuable and, ultimately, even leads to great joy:

> So be truly glad. There is wonderful joy ahead, even though you must endure many trials for a little while. These trials will show that your faith is genuine. It is being tested as fire tests and purifies gold—though your faith is far more precious than mere gold. So when your faith remains strong through many trials, it will bring you much praise and glory and honor on the day when Jesus Christ is revealed to the whole world. (1 Peter 1:6–7)

The wilderness is where we are refined and character is developed within us. It is in this furnace of affliction and persecution that the truly godly person is made. Romans 5:3–4 says, "We can rejoice, too, when we run into problems and trials, for we know that they help us develop endurance. And endurance develops strength of character."

God's approval on David's life was because he was a man after the heart of God, not a man after a kingdom! King Saul never went through a purifying wilderness; therefore, he remained un-refined and insecure. David, however, was purified in the wilderness, and God even used Saul to send him there!

God's ways may be mysterious, but His plans are always good!

A Dream Deferred?

Refining can be painful, though. I won't mislead you—the wilderness is not a trip to Disneyland. Suffering is suffering—and it sometimes hits us in very painful ways.

God may have shown you dreams and visions of what He has called you to do. He may have spoken to you of the plans that He has for you. In the wilderness, however, it often seems that the more you seek the Lord and obey His Word, the further you get from the dream He has put in your heart.

Consider Joseph: He was given a dream of leadership—even his brothers and family would be under his authority. What came next? He was hurled into a pit by those who were supposed to protect him—his older brothers—and, shortly afterward, sold into slavery in a foreign land. Can you imagine the shock, disappointment, and pain?

It's almost certain he imagined that God would perform a miraculous intervention to free him quickly. These hopes would eventually fade because his slavery didn't last a few months or even a few years, but spanned more than ten years. That's a long time! All the while, he knew that those who had instigated his pain were living in freedom and enjoying the prosperity of their very wealthy father.

What did Joseph do? What was his response in his desert

season? He kept his faith, served, and didn't forget God's promise. He was faithful, wise, diligent and, as a result, experienced a blessed success.

However, his conditions would again suddenly change and become far worse. His boss's wife cast longing eyes on Joseph. She sought to entice him into adultery, not just once or twice, but on multiple occasions. Even so, Joseph obeyed God and fled from sexual immorality every time. Finally, the woman became so aggressive that Joseph literally had to run away from her clutches. She, now scorned, falsely accused him of the very thing he didn't do. He was unfairly "convicted" and hurled into a dungeon. (Typically, a foreign slave attempting to rape a king's officer's wife would never see the light of day again.)

A person in prison gets a lot of time to reflect. Can you imagine the thoughts Joseph had to fight off? *I've served God faithfully all my life, and what has that gotten me? It turns out, by no fault of my own, I'm in this dungeon to rot away. My life is over! My wicked brothers are free and most likely enjoying great abundance. What have I done wrong? All I did was share my supposed "God-given" dream with my brothers and look what it got me! What good is it that I've served God?! It seems the more I obey Him, the worse life gets for me.*

Who could fault Joseph for having these thoughts? They seem like sound logic, right?

Then one day in the dungeon, Joseph faced his greatest wilderness test. God brought two men to him, a butler and a baker, who each had a dream that left him confused and seeking an interpretation. If Joseph would have lost faith in God and His promise, it would have been quite easy to be self-focused and blow them off. He could have said, "You had dreams last night? Hah, I once had a dream, too. I also thought the dream came from God. But here's the truth—dreams don't come to pass. Dreams are useless, vain, and misleading. So, would you please just leave me alone?!"

If Joseph had done this, he would have remained in his wilderness for many more years or, perhaps, even the rest of his life. He would have bypassed his ticket to freedom (the butler later told the king of Joseph's ability to interpret dreams, which led to Joseph's release from prison and a promotion). If he had a self-pitying attitude, Joseph would have eventually died in that dungeon a bitter, cynical, and hopeless man—expressing in various ways, "God isn't faithful; He doesn't keep His promises!"

But this is not what Joseph did. He fought off the thoughts and logic that were contrary to his personal promise from God and chose to serve the butler and baker. He stayed consistent in his obedience to God. And the outcome? Eventually he went free and was promoted in one day to become second in command to Pharaoh!

Nine years after Joseph's promotion to leadership, the circumstances of a severe famine resulted in his brothers coming to Egypt and standing before him. Joseph's course of action wasn't revenge, as most would have chosen. He now had the character of a true kingdom leader. He did good to those who did him evil. He was not a bitter man, but a man full of faith, love, and forgiveness for the ones who had betrayed him. The Psalmist writes about Joseph:

> He [God] sent a man before them—Joseph—who was sold
> as a slave. They hurt his feet with fetters, he was laid in

irons. Until the time that *His Word* came to pass, the Word
of the LORD tested him. (Psalm 105:17–19 NKJV)

Only God knew the set time that His personal promise to Joseph would come to pass (over twenty years after the dream). The
wilderness forged in him the character that would build his life,
family, and leadership position well. The key to all his success was
his reverential fear of the Lord. No matter his conditions, Joseph
would speak, act, and obey God's Word.

Now, what about you? As previously pointed out, God may
have shown you dreams and visions of what He has called you to
do. He may have spoken to you of the plans that He has for you.
But just as with Joseph, you are in a wilderness and it seems that
the more you seek the Lord and obey His Word, the further you
get from the dream He put in your heart.

You may have watched others, even those who've been adver-
sarial to your cause, be promoted in ministry (or any other arena
of life), while you seem to be going in the opposite direction of
your God-given dream. You may be doing everything you know
to do, but the vision is not becoming reality.

There may even be others around you who are carnal and not
seeking the Lord, but they are being promoted and appear to be
prospering. They are the ones receiving the financial and social
"blessings." There may be people who are advancing because of
their own flattery or manipulation. There may be people who are
doing things dishonestly, achieving success by lying and cheating,
yet still it appears they are "blessed," while you are like Joseph, in
chains in Pharaoh's dungeon.

What are you doing about it? Are you complaining? Look what God says:

> "You have said terrible things about Me," says the LORD. "But you say, 'What do you mean? What have we said against you?' "You have said, 'What's the use of serving God? What have we gained by obeying His commands or by trying to show the LORD of Heaven's Armies that we are sorry for our sins? From now on we will call the arrogant (wicked) blessed. For those who do evil get rich, and those who dare God to punish them suffer no harm.'" (Malachi 3:13–15)

What are the complainers saying here? They're saying, "What profit is it that we've obeyed God, because we're going nowhere. It is the wicked—the carnal, the impostors—not us, who are promoted, blessed, and prosper" (this is the "Bevere Paraphrase"). God calls this terrible or harsh talk, and He views it as being directed against Him. More plainly put, it is murmuring and complaining.

Complaining kept the children of Israel from their promised land. Why is complaining an affront to God, and why did it meet a stern judgment? It indirectly says to God, "I don't like what You are doing in my life and if I were You, I would do it differently." It is a complete lack of reverence for Him.

God is finding out who is going to pursue Him and who is going to pursue the benefits. The former are resolute in their pursuit; the latter will complain when things aren't right in their eyes. What some *call* blessings and what *really* are blessings are two different things. Some blessings may not last if your attitude (heart) is not right. To those with selfish motives who complain, look what the Lord says He will do to them, as well as to their blessings:

> "Listen, you priests [complaining believers]—this command is for you! Listen to Me and make up your minds to honor My Name," says the LORD of Heaven's Armies, "or I will bring a terrible curse against you. I will curse even the blessings you receive. Indeed, I have already cursed them, because you have not taken My warning to heart." (Malachi 2:1–2)

Our reward or inheritance does not consist of things or positions. Our inheritance is the Lord!

Ezekiel 44:28 says, "It shall be, in regard to their inheritance, that I am their inheritance . . . I am their possession" (NKJV).

Many Christians today have gotten their eyes off of the *true* inheritance and instead focus on things or positions—perhaps even good things that were given by God. But it is like the son who is more interested in what his father gives him than in a relationship with his father. I have four sons, and I love to give to them. However, it would break my heart if the only reason they gave attention to me was to get from me what they wanted from me. Look at what Malachi goes on to say:

> Then those who feared the LORD spoke with each other, and the LORD listened to what they said. In His presence, a scroll of remembrance was written to record the names of those who feared Him and always thought about the honor of His Name. (Malachi 3:16)

These are the ones who are going through the same wilderness conditions as the "complainers," but this group's priority is not position, recognition, or things. They seek the heart of God! The desire to know Him burns in them. You can talk to them about social things or business things, but their heart burns when you talk to them about the Lord or what He is saying.

These are the ones about whom Luke says, "They said to each other, 'Didn't our hearts burn within us as He talked with us on the road and explained the Scriptures to us?'" (Luke 24:32). Their desires are *set* on the things of the Spirit. They are saying, "I just want to know God; I want to please Him; I hunger and thirst for the Word of the Lord; I want Him to take joy in me for He is the source of my joy." That's what matters most. Their first love is Jesus, not position, status, or possessions.

Their behavior is not altered by whether they are in the middle of the desert or preaching to millions.

> For we are God's fellow workers; you are God's field, you are God's building. According to the grace of God which was given me, as a wise master builder I have laid the foundation, and another builds on it. But let each one take heed how he builds on it. (1 Corinthians 3:9–10 NKJV)

We need to pay careful attention to how we build our lives! In Scripture, the building of a house symbolizes the building of our life and service to the kingdom. We belong to God; for we are His building:

. . . Christ Jesus, who was faithful to Him who appointed Him, as Moses also was faithful in all His house. For this One has been counted worthy of more glory than Moses, inasmuch as He who built the house has more honor than the house. For every house is built by someone, but He who built all things is God. (Hebrews 3:1–4 NKJV)

Notice who builds the house—the Lord. It is not the strength of our flesh. Whatever God builds remains; what we build will not. "Unless the LORD builds the house, they labor in vain who build it" (Psalm 127:1 NKJV). What man builds apart from God—whether it is his life, home, or even a ministry—it will not endure.

In Genesis 11:4 we see an example of this: "Come, let us build ourselves a city, and a tower whose top is in the heavens; let us make a name for ourselves" (NKJV).

What was the motive of those who built the tower of Babel? They wanted to achieve their self-seeking dreams, to raise their edifice for their own glory. They wanted to be like God, but totally independent of Him. That pursuit fulfilled their desires and their will, but not God's. Building apart from God never works out, because no matter how noble our intent, without God it is an exercise in futility. This is why we are warned:

But let each one take heed how he builds on it. . . . Now if anyone builds on this foundation [which is Christ Jesus] with gold, silver, precious stones, wood, hay, straw, each one's work will become clear; for the Day ["who can endure the day of His coming?"] will declare it, because it will be revealed by fire; and the fire will test each one's work, of what sort it is. (1 Corinthians 3:10–13 NKJV)

Gold, silver, and precious stones represent construction God's way. Wood, hay, and straw represent our own methods of construction by the blueprint of the world. Are these verses talking only about judgment in heaven? No! The verses describe when He comes to His temple (Malachi 3:16–4:1 and 1 Corinthians 3:16–17). He will come as fire, which will either *consume* wood, hay, and straw or *refine* gold and silver. That is why He goes on to say, "If anyone's work is burned, he will suffer loss; but he himself will be saved, yet so as through fire" *(verse 15 NKJV).*

If you build your life, business, or ministry with bricks of your own making, such as the strength of your personality or by worldly programs or techniques . . . if you build by manipulating or controlling people through intimidation . . . if you flatter and ride the coattails of others to gain position . . . if when building you tear down others through criticism or gossip . . . then everything gained by these methods will be burned up and lost.

Many promote themselves, using deceptive techniques or even bold lying to gain advantage. This, too, will be burned! "Let no one deceive himself. If anyone among you seems to be wise in this age, let him become a fool that he may become wise. For the wisdom of this world is foolishness with God" (1 Corinthians 3:18–19 NKJV).

In God's eyes, any area of your life in which your motive is self-seeking, is considered wood, hay, or straw. Regardless of how much it appears to help others or operates in the name of the Lord or is time sacrificed, it all burns.

The focus of this world's wisdom is self. "But if you have bitter envy and self-seeking in your hearts . . . . This wisdom does not descend from above, but is earthly, sensual, demonic" (James 3:14–15 NKJV). Envy begets competition and suspicion. In order to keep our domain safe, we may begin to play power games, which may cost us friends and our integrity or, most importantly, damage our relationship with God. Even pastors or others in ministry may become driven by the concerns of position, title, or salary at the expense of living close to God's heart.

For others who genuinely seek God's heart, it may seem like the more they seek Him, the more they move away. In frustration they cry out:

> "God, the more I seek You, the more I go down, not up."
> But God answers, "Dig deeper!"
> "Whoever comes to Me, and hears My sayings and does them, I will show you whom he is like: he is like a man building a house, who dug deep and laid the foundation on the rock. . . ." (Luke 6:47–48 NKJV)

When our family lived in Dallas, I would watch builders erect skyscrapers. At first the progress was slow, as months were devoted to breaking rock and digging for the foundation. The bigger the building, the deeper the hole and the more extensive the building's foundation. From above the ground, it seemed the builders were moving slowly and making little headway. Then, all of a sudden, the tall building would go up rapidly. Its progress would seem to occur almost overnight compared to the preparation process.

The *upward progression* was nothing when compared with the *downward preparation*.

I believe there are many in the body of Christ in the process of downward preparation—especially, perhaps, among the younger generation. I praise God for that! They may have a call to ministry or some other dream given by the Lord, but are presently in serving positions. Things don't appear to be moving very quickly, but I believe they are under God's careful preparation in the wilderness. The foundation is being laid; the character of Christ is being formed. This character will undergird all who will serve Christ and His kingdom with fervor in the years to come.

Others who are not dwelling in the wilderness appear to be moving swiftly upward through politics or some type of self-promotion. Our wilderness sojourners may feel they are at a standstill and may even be tempted to take the quick and easy route out themselves. But knowing that such a route yields no enduring character and that it compromises the existing character they already have attained, they decide the risk is too great. By waiting on God, they allow the Master Builder to lay a solid foundation on the Rock.

Presently, there are pastors diligently seeking God, but again it appears very little to even nothing is happening. They are in a dry place or time. They watch as others promote themselves and their ministries successfully through the use of secular marketing techniques. They create illusions of happiness and success on social media. Yet God will not allow these desert sojourners to build through these methods, because He is preparing their solid, lasting foundation.

Then there are those whom God has not yet shown a particular position or place, but He has given them a dream. They are wondering how it will ever come to pass, and its possible fulfillment appears to be slipping away.

Survival Tips for Your Journey

#8 Joshua Got It Right

If the wilderness is intended for our good, how do we lay hold of the good and avoid the bad?

Joshua is a good example of someone whose heart was correct in the wilderness. When Moses went up to Mt. Sinai, Joshua stayed at the mountain's foot. He wanted to get as close as possible to the presence of the Lord. When Moses met with God in the tabernacle, Joshua was there also, in order to be close to the presence of the Lord. Even when Moses was finished, Joshua remained in the Tent of Meeting (Exodus 33:11).

In the book of Joshua, we see that the five areas of sin that plagued their parents (the previous generation) did not manifest themselves as readily with the second (Joshua's) generation in the wilderness. It did happen once with a man named Achan. However, the leadership and people immediately sought God to take care of it. The second generation got it right because they had watched the failures of the prior generation—how their parents had all died in the wilderness without seeing God's promise fulfilled.

Joshua and his generation kept their focus on the Creator, and they entered the Promised Land. They were strong in keeping God's Word and they stayed free from discouragement. They refused to complain; they were quick to believe God.

In this dry or wilderness time, God separates those who will wait on Him in obedience from those who will build with the tools of deception or calculated self-promoting behavior or manipulation. True God-ordained promotion—and an exit from the wilderness—will come to those who are watching and waiting for God to come to His temple. He says:

> "When I choose the proper time, I will judge uprightly." . . . For exaltation comes neither from the east nor from the west nor from the south. But God is the Judge: He puts down one, and exalts another." (Psalm 75:2–7 NKJV)

Futility of the Flesh

The truth of the struggle between flesh and Spirit applies to all aspects of life, not just ministry endeavors. Remember, flesh can never bring forth God's promises! If something is birthed by the flesh—good luck with that! Flesh will have to sustain it. If the Spirit births it, God will provide for it.

The flesh scenario usually leads to an environment of manipulation and control. Leaders will exert power or play on human emotions to get results. If you are one of their followers, all of a sudden you have become responsible for *their* success or failure, depending upon how you respond to their direction. There will be a lot of pressure, legalism, domination, or manipulation involved.

Even though I am primarily addressing ministry practices, I want to emphasize that this is *not* just ministries; I'm describing *anything* created in the power of the flesh. So this can apply to our callings in the marketplace, education, healthcare, government, the military, professional athletics, and the many other arenas where God calls His people to serve.

Conversely, that born of the Spirit will understand that it had no role in its own formation, so it knows it cannot maintain or cause growth by its own ability. The responsibility will be on God to provide for that which He created (or built).

When Isaac was born, Ishmael's position was already well-established (Genesis 16–21). In my experience, I have found that the opportunity for an Ishmael endeavor will always present itself before the promised Isaac dream is birthed. The temptation to use your own strength to bring forth what God promised you *must* be resisted. Recall again the verse, "'Get rid of that slave woman and her son. He is not going to share the inheritance with my son, Isaac. I won't have it!'" (Genesis 21:10).

The day is coming when the Lord shall say to His people, "Cast out the Ishmael endeavors, for the offspring of the flesh shall have no inheritance with the offspring of promise." Even though they appear to be productive, God will say, "Cast them out!" so that no flesh will have glory in His presence!

When God's judgment is revealed, any portion of your life that has been built by your own ability will not survive the refining fire. If you build your life totally through efforts of self-preservation and self-promotion, then all of it will burn. But you "will be saved, yet so as through fire" (1 Corinthians 3:15 NKJV).

The only things that will remain are those that are received by promise, conceived and birthed through God's Spirit and grace.

9

STRENGTH TRAINING

The Lord gets His best soldiers out of the highlands of affliction.

—Charles H. Spurgeon

So the child grew and became strong in spirit, and was in the deserts till the day of his manifestation to Israel.

—Luke 1:80 (NKJV)

Some years ago, I endured a different type of challenge that illustrates how, as followers of Christ, we need times of preparation that stretch us and strengthen our faith. Believe it or not, this trial took place not in some dry, barren desert, but in gyms and health clubs.

When I was thirty-five years old, after preaching my heart out at a church in Atlanta, Georgia, I almost fainted on the platform. I realized that I was not in good physical shape and knew I needed to get stronger if I was to forge ahead faithfully in ministry.

I returned home from Georgia and told Lisa what had happened. I then declared, "I'm going to the gym."

To my surprise, her answer was, "Thank God. I've been praying for you to go to the gym!" It's really wonderful to have a wife who knows how to pray for her husband!

We were living in Florida at the time, and two houses down from us was a WWF wrestler named Kip. Our families had become close, as our children were approximately the same age. He had offered a number of times to take me to the gym and train me, but I'd always said, "No, I'm too busy. I don't have time." I was busy, but also a bit intimidated—would you want to train with a professional wrestler?

Kip was a massive guy, six feet four inches, 240 pounds, six percent body fat. His chest was a perfect V and he had an eight pack. Frequently, he, our kids, and I played driveway basketball or street hockey. If I ran into him, he didn't even budge, and I would go flying five or six feet back!

After that Atlanta trip, I walked down to his house and said, "Kip, I need to go to the gym. You've been saying you would train me—would you still like to do that?"

He quickly answered, "Sure, I'll take you to the gym." I should have paid more attention to his sadistic smile. I had no idea what was in store for me!

The next morning, we both went to a sweatbox of a gym. Immediately, I knew that only the serious people trained at this place. The atmosphere was surging with testosterone and the body odor was overpowering. One of the things I learned at the gym on that first day was that you don't build muscle by putting a light weight on the bar and pushing it up twenty or thirty times. Instead, you put a lot of weight on the bar so that you can only push it up three or four times.

It's on that third or fourth rep all the good things start happening to your muscles. This is when everything in you says, "I can't lift it anymore!" But with all the guys around your bench screaming, "Push, push, explode!" something else inside causes you to give it all you've got and lift the weight up that fourth or fifth time. To make a very complex matter simply understood, that's when real muscle is developed.

Well, I'm embarrassed to say that all I could bench press that first day was 95 pounds. I'm sure Kip knew then that his neighbor had a long way to go! After a couple of weeks at the gym, I made it to 105 pounds. More weeks passed and I lifted 115. Then I arrived at 125 pounds. When I finally got up to 135, I was so proud that I could now put a plate—a standard 45-pound weight—on each side of the bar. I didn't lift in shame any longer.

There's more to this story that I'll share later in the chapter, but my process of slowly gaining physical strength is a good analogy to what happens when the Lord takes us to His "gym" in the wilderness and helps us gain spiritual muscle.

It's in the wilderness where our spirit becomes strong, because it's a place—not only of dryness and crying out, "God, where are You?!"—but also a place of profound trial and temptation. The good news is that although the wilderness is tough and challenging, we must remember who is pulling for us to lift the weight during our spiritual strength training:

If God is for us, who can ever be against us? (Romans 8:31)

Not only is He for us and pulling for us, but He makes us a firm promise:

You can trust God, who will not permit you to be tempted more than you can stand. (1 Corinthians 10:13 NCV)

So, no matter what test you're facing, whatever bleak, dry place you are walking through, God promises us that we will never be in a temptation that we don't have the strength to get through successfully. It's quite amazing when you think about it.

As you face trials, never forget who you are. As a beloved child of God, Jesus says, "Behold, I give you the authority . . . over all the power of the enemy, and nothing shall by any means hurt you" (Luke 10:19 NKJV). And so, we realize that no matter what the enemy throws at us, we can overcome it. If not, God wouldn't permit it!

However, this is where the problem also lies. Many people do not grow in their ability to handle greater challenges. They avoid the gym, so to speak, or whine and complain once there. Yet Paul illustrates a totally different attitude. He writes:

> "For to you *it has been granted* on behalf of Christ, not only to believe in Him, but also to suffer for His sake." (Philippians 1:29 NKJV)

Does it make you scratch your head a little when you read that suffering has been "granted" to you? What does this really mean? When somebody says to me, "It has been granted," that sounds like a blessing is coming my way. Expectantly I think—*just what am I going to receive?*

How can "granted" and "suffering" be in the same sentence? That's like saying to somebody, "For to you it is granted on your birthday to go to the dentist for a root canal!" *Really? Thanks, but no thanks.* This just doesn't make sense, because the life we desire in a modern country like the United States is one of comfort and relative ease. So being granted "suffering" can mess with your mind. Most people when they encounter adversity say things like, "I can't believe this is happening to me."

"Why me?"

"Why do I have to go through this?"

"I hate this."

"No one can relate to what I'm going through!"

"Why can't I just have a normal life?"

"God, please take this away!"

"Why bother? Giving up would be easier . . ."

At times, I'm certain all of us have either thought or expressed attitudes like these when facing adversity. Sad to say, too often we just don't understand the purpose of trials and suffering (the wilderness).

But, as always, God knows what we need—and what strength we need in order to build up to have greater effectiveness for His kingdom's efforts. So, this is why Paul informs us of God's promise that some strategic suffering to increase our faith muscles is "going to be granted."

The Role of Temptation

As I mentioned earlier, part of our wilderness strength training includes growing in our ability to recognize and resist temptation. Jesus experienced this early in His ministry when the Father permitted the devil to tempt Him in the wilderness: "Then Jesus, being filled with the Holy Spirit, returned from the Jordan and was led by the Spirit into the wilderness, being tempted for forty days by the devil" (Luke 4:1–2 NKJV).

I carefully chose the word "permitted," because God is never the author of temptation: "Let no one say when he is tempted, 'I

am tempted by God'; for God cannot be tempted by evil, nor does
He Himself tempt anyone" (James 1:13 NKJV).

What is really happening to us when we are tempted? We
know that Satan's intention is to cause us to fall into sin and, as a
result, move us away from our joyful obedience and relationship
with God. So, if Satan wants that as a result of his temptation,
what is God seeking by allowing us to be tempted? The apostle
Peter offers this insight: "Therefore, since Christ suffered for us
in the flesh, arm yourselves also with the same mind, for he who
has suffered in the flesh has ceased from sin" (1 Peter 4:1 NKJV).

In other words, this testing via temptation, this conquering of
sin and other issues in the wilderness, is to help us build up our
spiritual muscle and become increasingly mature. In this verse,
the key words are "arm yourselves."

Can you imagine a military unit going into battle without
being armed? No gunships, no tanks, no rifles, no ammunition—
no arms at all? That would be a disaster. That is the same kind of
disaster a Christ follower faces when they are not armed to suffer,
when they are not armed for trials.

Commercial airline pilots are a good example of those who are
armed for a possible test. Every six months, the airline sends them
for recurrent training. These pilots have to go into a simulator and
respond effectively to every imaginable worst-case scenario. What
is intended is the strengthening of each pilot's ability to know how
to handle an emergency situation. Typically in an airline crisis, the
passengers—who definitely are *not armed*—are reacting, while the
pilot is acting. Why? Because the pilot has been *armed*.

That's what the wilderness does for an obedient Christian. It confronts us with adversity that serves to arm us for future conquests. We must realize that adversity—the wilderness—is going to happen to us. Jesus said in this world we're going to face troubles and tribulation, but He will help us overcome them. And in this process, we will be strengthened.

The Great Opportunity

Our attitude toward the wilderness should be to see it as a great opportunity to build spiritual muscle, to get stronger for what the Lord wants to give us next. Here's what the apostle James says:

Survival Tips for Your Journey

#9 Don't Create an Ishmael

When we find ourselves in the wilderness and think we've camped there way too long, the temptation will come to "just do something" to bring on the dream. I call this the birthing of an Ishmael, which happens when we try to do through our own efforts what God promised us He'd do. Ishmaels are often born of a legitimate need but are birthed by flesh.

Of course, this idea originates with the story of Abraham and Sarah, to whom God had promised a son. They had waited for eleven years and, my goodness, Abraham was 86 and Sarah was way too old to have a baby. So they went to Plan B—Sarah suggested that Abraham take Hagar and get the promised child through her. This was

Dear brothers and sisters, when troubles of any kind come your way, consider it an opportunity . . . . (James 1:2)

All of us should understand opportunity because as Americans, we celebrate entrepreneurs. An opportunity in business, for example, is a chance to grow, to succeed, to prosper. It's a chance to expand our horizons. And that's exactly the way troubles are to be viewed, because James goes on to say, "For you know that when your faith is tested, your endurance has a chance to grow. So let it grow, for when your endurance is fully developed, you will be perfect and complete, needing nothing" (James 1:3-4).

---

a very bad idea. And every Ishmael approach—even if it looks kind of good—is also a bad idea. Always remember, what you birth by the strength of your flesh, you will have to sustain by the strength of your flesh!

In some of my wilderness stays, I've tried a Plan B. I knew God had promised me that someday I'd have a global preaching ministry. But it wasn't happening—I was "stuck" in local church ministry. So I tried a few times to force my hand and escape the wilderness. My efforts came at a price and nothing panned out. Once I broke, God eventually made His move and it all turned around.

I urge you—save yourself the heartache and don't create an Ishmael. Let God bring forth what He promised to you.

In the wilderness we are granted the opportunity to *grow our endurance*. How do we use the word "endurance" most frequently in today's world? I hear it often related to endurance training, which is defined as the deliberate act of exercising to increase our stamina. Simply put, endurance training enlarges our *capacity* to handle future challenges.

So, here's the situation: In any trials we face, God allows these hardships for a purpose, and that purpose is to produce *capacity*. God will permit, and again I emphasize the word *permit*, a hardship today that's going to simulate (recall the pilot's flight simulator) the levels of pressure He knows we're going to face tomorrow. That's why a trial always feels greater than our current level of preparedness or responsibility. So the bottom line is that God is using our present challenges to strengthen us for greater conquests in our future.

Now back to my weight-lifting challenge. As I've already shared, Kip had trained me to the point where I could lift 135 pounds. Even though for me this was a great achievement, I wondered, could I do more? In comparing my weight training to spiritual readiness and strength, what if the Lord had a task waiting for me that required more strength than lifting 135 pounds?

So, I kept going to the gym. I finally lifted 205 pounds but got stuck at that weight for a couple of years. I was speaking at a conference in California and some guys there said to me, "John, you've never lifted 225 pounds?"

"No, I've been trying for over five years," I said, with some disappointment.

"We'll help you break through," they said. And sure enough, that day I pushed up to 225. I was so excited!

After this, a new team member joined our ministry, Messenger International. I learned that he had been a weight-lifting competitor, so he and I started training together. With his help, I actually was able to lift 235 pounds, and once even pushed up 245. But could I go higher?

A year later, I preached at a church in Detroit. After the services on Sunday, the pastor said, "John, I've got a trainer. He's a nationally renowned weight trainer who attends our church. My appointment's tomorrow morning. Do you want to come with me?"

"Sure!" I said with great excitement.

We went the next day. The trainer sized me up and asked a question: "So, the most you've pushed up is 245?"

"Yeah, but it was only once."

"Well, today we're going to do more than that."

What?! I didn't want to say it, but I was thinking, *You're nuts. There's no way!"* But after some coaching and training, unbelievably, he got me to push up 265 pounds.

I was super excited. He sent my team member and me back to Colorado and each week this trainer coached us through email. We kept working hard at it, and the next year I returned to the same church in Detroit. By this time, I was 42 years old.

I preached that Sunday on the marvelous attributes of the Holy Spirit. Monday came and we all went to the same gym. The trainer said, "John, I had a dream last night that you pushed up over 300 pounds."

"That is absolutely crazy!" I said. What I probably was thinking—*Good for you, but I didn't have a dream like that!*

"John, you preached yesterday on the power of the Holy

Spirit. He gave me that dream last night! Get down on that bench. We're going to do this!"

And so, after warmups, the weights were loaded on the bar, and with a mighty grunt I pushed up 325 pounds!

I was so excited I called Lisa from the Detroit airport and said, "I don't need a plane to fly home—I am on such a high right now!"

At that time when I lifted the 325, I was routinely lifting 225 pounds. In fact, I could do sets where I lifted that weight ten times. But, recall what I was doing when I started seven years earlier. What would have happened to me, if at age 35, Kip had put 225 pounds on that bar instead of 95? I could have been killed! The bar with all the weight would have fallen and crushed me! It had taken me years of consistent effort to arrive at my current strength. So what was now considered routine weight would have been my end seven years earlier!

This is why the trials we go through, often in many situations over long periods of time, actually are spiritual strength training that helps prepare us for even greater tests in the future. When we are stronger in the Lord, we have the ability to do more in building the kingdom.

A sad thing is that there will be people who stand before the judgment seat and with tears in His eyes, Jesus will say to them, "I had so much more for you to do, but you didn't have the *capacity* to handle the challenges that came with it." This is particularly tragic because, as we know, God will never give us more than He knows we can handle. It's His promise to us!

So let's use my weight lifting story as an analogy. If you're able to lift a 135-pound spiritual challenge, and God has a plan or position that requires the *capacity* to lift 185 pounds of opposition, persecution, temptation, and trials, He won't permit it—you're just not strong enough. Instead, He will allow the training process to commence. He will permit—He won't *author*—perhaps a 155-pound trial that will further test, but not overwhelm you.

For example, maybe somebody gossips about you and spreads a rumor. Instead of countering the attack by defending yourself and spreading gossip about that person, you, in obedience to God's Word, choose to say nothing and bless instead. That's great—you lifted the 155-pound test! Now it's on to the next level: 165 pounds. If you continue to obey His Word through the adversities, your training continues until you arrive at the 185-pound level. You are now prepared for this higher plan or new position in the kingdom, which is God's plan for your life.

But if you respond to the gossip by getting offended and lashing back at the person—you guessed it—the Lord weeps and says, "I'm sorry, but you need to go back and lift some more 145-pound challenges." You're still in the "gym" but not benefiting from it.

The training continues but at the same level. Next He permits financial trouble—another 155-pound test—to come against you. But instead of seeking God's provision, you immediately say, "No problem! Our credit card's not maxed out!" And God takes off the extra weight and says, "Back to 145."

The time will eventually come when God needs you for that particular kingdom task or position that carries 185 pounds of opposition. If wilderness tests—the weight training—are continually failed, He can't invite you in because you don't have the spiritual muscle to lift the adversity in that situation or position. This is when He must find someone other than you to handle the task or take the position.

Greater Authority and Power

This is why the wilderness is so important: *It builds our strength.*

In the wilderness, John the Baptist became strong in spirit.

In the wilderness, Jesus became strong in spirit.

Their spiritual muscles were developed, not in the easy times, but in the times when the trials came, when their faith was tested.

Here is the good news from James . . . when you come through a trial, and you do it God's way, you will be wonderfully ready—*strong*—for what God has next for you:

> For you know that when your faith is tested, your endurance has a chance to grow. So let it grow, for when your endurance is fully developed, you will be perfect and complete, needing nothing. (James 1:3–4)

When James says, "So let it grow," the *it* is our capacity and our endurance. James also tells us what we can look forward to if we embrace the wilderness: "God blesses those who patiently endure testing and temptation. Afterward they will receive the crown of life that God has promised to those who love Him" (James 1:12).

The word "crown" conveys authority, and with authority comes power. Just as Jesus went into the wilderness to be tempted by the devil and through His obedience and perseverance came out with greater authority and power (see Luke 4:1, 14), we too can emerge from wilderness seasons with greater authority and power.

I don't know about you, but I want to be sure I have the spiritual muscle to handle what the Lord has prepared for me.

"Gym anybody?"

10

WATER IN THE WILDERNESS

If we cannot believe God when circumstances seem to be against us, we do not believe Him at all.

—Charles H. Spurgeon

"Those who drink the water I give will never be thirsty again. It becomes a fresh, bubbling spring within them, giving them eternal life."

—John 4:13–14

Rain is scarce in the desert. Water is not accessed easily there, and if it is to be found at all, it must be drawn from wells or springs. The wilderness is a dry and thirsty land (Psalm 63:1 NKJV). Therefore, Jesus invites us with these words:

> "If anyone thirsts, let him come to Me and drink. He who
> believes in Me, as the Scripture has said, out of his heart
> will flow rivers of living water." But this He spoke concern-
> ing the Spirit. . . (John 7:37–39 NKJV)

I recall several instances in dry seasons when I would try to pray and found it difficult to get a refreshing drink of living water. One such time, while seeking the Lord, I took my tent to a state park to spend the evening and next morning. That night I prayed, then I read, then I began to sing songs of praise. I spent approximately three hours doing these things, and it seemed I was getting nowhere. Nothing seemed fresh—I was as dry as could be. Very disappointed, I finally crawled in my sleeping bag and tried to sleep.

During that night, it seemed as if all the demons were having a celebration—I didn't sleep very well. I tossed and turned, wondering why God was not manifesting Himself to me. The next morning I went outdoors and began walking the paths of the state park, praying in the Spirit, but still feeling very dry. This went on for another hour and a half. I finally looked up and said, "Lord, I guess I am in the wilderness." My thoughts were, *I might as well go home and quit seeking Him; He has me in this dry place, and things won't change until He brings me out.*

This was erroneous thinking! God does not bring us into these times to frustrate us and get us to give up until He sovereignly changes our conditions! The wilderness is not intended to be a place of failure, but of victory! All of a sudden, I heard a still, small voice within me say, "*Fight!*" That one small word was the spark of fire and life that I needed. Immediately I said, "Stir up the gift of God in me! Come forth rivers of living water! Spring up, O well into my soul!" I had remembered what had happened when the Israelites were in the desert:

> From there the Israelites traveled to Beer, which is the well
> where the Lord said to Moses, "Assemble the people, and
> I will give them water." There the Israelites sang this song:
> "Spring up, O well!" (Numbers 21:16–17)

As I kept repeating these words found in Scripture, the prayer became more and more intense until I found myself pacing up and down that path, praying and speaking the Word of the Lord with great strength and fire. Everything became fresh and I was like a different person! His presence was with me in a strong way. Just minutes earlier I had felt heavy and weak, but now I was gearing up for battle, ready to face any enemy with the Word of the Lord!

This lasted about twenty-five minutes, but it seemed like only five. Now I was refreshed and ready to take on the world!

Jesus says that rivers or springs of living water will flow out of the heart of one who comes to Him and drinks. It is not the outpouring (rain) of the Spirit of God that we experience in the desert. In this dry place, the water of refreshing must be drawn deep from our heart, the fountain or well of God.

Notice that Jesus points out (John 7:39) that the well-source He's speaking of is the Spirit of the Lord, and that rivers (plural), not a river (singular), would flow out of a believer's heart.

How does the Spirit of the Lord flow like rivers from our heart? The prophet Isaiah explains the nature of the Spirit's works: "And the spirit of the LORD shall rest upon him, the spirit of wisdom and understanding, the spirit of counsel and might, the spirit of knowledge and of the fear of the LORD" (Isaiah 11:2 NKJV).

The Holy Spirit is called the Spirit of Wisdom, the Spirit of Understanding, the Spirit of Counsel, the Spirit of Might, the Spirit of Knowledge, and the Spirit of the Fear of the Lord. Since Jesus says that the Spirit would be as rivers, that means there's a river of Wisdom, a river of Understanding, a river of Counsel, a river of Might, a river of Knowledge, and a river of the Fear of the Lord. No wonder my heart caught fire on that path near my campsite!

Here are some more supporting truths:

- Proverb 18:4 says, "The words of a man's mouth are deep waters; the wellspring of wisdom is a flowing brook" (NKJV).
- Proverb 16:22 says, "Understanding is a wellspring of life to him who has it" (NKJV).

- Proverb 20:5 says, "Counsel in the heart of man is like deep water, but a man of understanding will draw it out" (NKJV).

These wells are found in the heart of a believer, because this is where the Spirit abides. However, it is only the person who understands the ways of the Lord who will draw the waters out of the well. The key word is "draw." Again, it is important to remember: The waters of refreshing in the wilderness do not come from the Spirit's rain but must be *drawn* from the heart.

- Proverb 10:11 says, "The mouth of the righteous is a well of life . . ." (NKJV).
- Proverb 15:23 says, "A man has joy by the answer of his mouth" (NKJV)

If I had chosen to walk away from that campsite saying, "I might as well go home and quit seeking Him; He has me in this dry place, and things won't change until He brings me out," I would have taken my heaviness with me. But because I spoke what God put into my heart, it gave me what was needed to draw from the deep wells. I had tapped into the underground pool of salvation and was drawing out the water of refreshment. It truly was like drinking cool water from a spring in the middle of the desert!

Many give up in these dry times, but God is saying, "Keep pressing onward; don't stop!" We must have a persistent and tenacious drive within us that won't let us quit until His will is accomplished.

Many stop praying when they feel dry; they stop because no water is coming from the wells, and it seems too difficult to obtain. They are weak, and God wants their strength built up for battles they will face in the future.

From where do we find the strength to draw? From joy! Isaiah 12:3 says, "Therefore with joy you will draw water from the wells of salvation" (NKJV). This is because "the joy of the LORD is your strength" (Nehemiah 8:10 NKJV). Joy is a spiritual force that strengthens us.

What is the joy of the Lord? For years I thought that the joy of the Lord was to have the joy that He has. I had a hard time relating to that. However, that is not what He is saying. Have you ever heard someone make a statement something like, "The joy of cooking"? Cooking has no joy in itself. What they are saying is that you will experience joy in cooking. The "joy of the Lord" is the joy we experience from our relationship with Him. He brings us joy!

Just because we don't feel His presence in the prayer closet does not mean He is denying us. Therefore, our joy is not based on how we feel. Rather, it's based on who He is and the privilege we have of being related to Him. So, we see past the lies of being denied and instead realize He is drawing us . . . toward the deep wells!

Unstopping the Wells

Abraham's miracle son, Isaac, once found himself in a time of dryness:

> A severe famine now struck the land, as had happened before in Abraham's time. . . . The LORD appeared to Isaac and said, "Do not go down to Egypt, but do as I tell you. Live here as a foreigner in this land, and I will be with you and bless you." (Genesis 26:1–3)

God specifically tells Isaac not to run to Egypt where it is comfortable, but to stay where God had put him. Many times when we find ourselves in a dry place, the first thing we think is, "I'm getting out of here!" If in a time of morning prayer, we are not sensing God's presence, our mind will start to wander as we think of all the things we need to do in the upcoming day. We will hastily conclude our prayer time and start processing our to-do list.

If it seems dry to us in the church we attend, without even asking God we determine, *I'm going to where there's some spiritual excitement and great preaching!*

Or if it seems dry in our social or business life, we consider leaving and finding a city with a booming economy. We think, *If I stay here, I'll dry up and never see the plan of God fulfilled in my life.*

There are so many American Christians who think these things. They run from one social media platform to another, activity to activity, from church to church, from city to city trying to find a place that is not dry. Instead of digging the wells and allowing God to use them to bring refreshing water to the dry place where they are, they "move to Egypt," so to speak, seeking relief and ease. What they don't understand is that in many of these dry times God intends to bring forth the vision He has given them. I know this may not always be the case, because there are times when God prepares us for a new place and allows the old to dry up. The key is to be led by the Spirit of God! If He is not saying anything, then stay and fight!

Look at what happens to Isaac as a result of obeying God and staying in that land of famine:

When Isaac planted his crops that year, he harvested a hundred times more grain than he planted, for the Lord blessed him. He became a very rich man, and his wealth continued to grow. He acquired so many flocks of sheep and goats,

Survival Tips for Your Journey

#10 The Secret Joy Medicine

When you're in a wilderness time, it's very easy to get your eyes locked in on your circumstances. I want to let you in on a little secret—seriously, this has helped me survive and thrive in desert times. I call it my Secret Joy Medicine.

When there's not a lot to be excited about on my outside, when it just seems like nothing's happening, maybe I've been praying and praying but not seeing any results, I go back to thinking about what Jesus did. I remember that He literally saved me out of a hell where the fire never stops burning and the sulfur odor never stops smelling. The torment there never ends. That hell wasn't created for me, but for the devil. But the devil tricked mankind and is bringing mankind there with him. Yet Jesus gave His life— my Creator gave *His* life to save *me* from that.

When I do this, when I get my eyes on Him, when I move into this perspective that is based on gratitude, when I look at life with this eternal view, all of a sudden my particular situation does not seem so significant. That's my Secret Joy Medicine—reviewing all the things I have to be thankful for and keeping my eyes on Jesus.

herds of cattle, and servants that the Philistines became jealous of him. So the Philistines filled up all of Isaac's wells with dirt. These were the wells that had been dug by the servants of his father, Abraham. . . . He reopened the wells his father had dug, which the Philistines had filled in after Abraham's death. Isaac also restored the names Abraham had given them. (Genesis 26:12–15, 18)

The water Isaac needed for his crops to grow was obtained by redigging his father's wells—the ones plugged up by the Philistines. Just as with Isaac, the water we so desperately need for the growth of God's incorruptible seed to mature in our hearts must often be drawn from stopped-up wells. The Philistines were of the world and its system. Often when we get too close to the system of this world, unknowingly our wells get plugged up. It is critical to unstop our wells so we can receive the needed watering of our souls.

I believe that the invasion of cultural values into the body of Christ today has "stopped up" many wells. Has the church that is intended to be a source of flowing water become a dry place because it has allowed the enemy to seduce it—to stop up wells?

The question we should ask is whether God can restore His church with fresh water? The answer: of course! This is the picture revealed so beautifully by Isaiah:

> The Lord will guide you continually,
>   giving you water when you are dry
>   and restoring your strength.
> You will be like a well-watered garden,
>   like an ever-flowing spring.

Some of you will rebuild the deserted ruins of your cities.
> Then you will be known as a rebuilder of walls
> and a restorer of homes. (Isaiah 58:11–12)

As Isaac did not seek his own way or pleasure by going to the land of ease, so we (by not doing things our way, seeking our own pleasure, or living on our own words but rather honoring God) shall be like a watered garden and a spring of living water whose waters do not fail! If we do things His way, through us God will bring His living water to dry and thirsty people.

God is leading us to redig any wells that the world has plugged up. Again, that takes persistence, and it may take longer than a few hours, days, weeks, months, or even years.

Loss of Passion

I believe I've made clear in this book that the wilderness is a metaphor for a huge array of circumstances. The common denominator is that we find ourselves in situations experiencing some type of deprivation or dryness. Often, a signal of a wilderness is the decline or total disappearance of our enthusiasm and passion for our calling or even for our relationship with God.

Let me briefly review my second significant wilderness experience while serving as a youth pastor.

The first nine months at the church in Florida were just fantastic—the ministry was expanding and the group was growing. I was excited and full of energy and passion. But then, seemingly out of the blue, the plug got pulled and all my passion and drive drained away.

I was spending more time in prayer than I had before and still it seemed I was getting nowhere. Not only that, the vision I had for the youth group seemed to be fading (the old wine was being poured out). The more I prayed, the more the vision dwindled. Nothing had changed outwardly, but inwardly something was changing.

On top of it all, in the midst of all this, we went through external trials like we had never experienced before. The biggest trial? My direct overseer was building a case to get me fired. His son was in our group and came to my wife one night after youth service and said, "Mrs. Lisa, how can I live the life John is preaching when my parents are doing . . . at home?" (There's no need to mention their specific behavior, other than to say it was not good.)

She was shocked and wisely counseled, "You stay true to the Word of God and leave the care of your parents with God." From that day forward, my boss set out to destroy my reputation and get rid of me. He launched a subtle, but all-out attack. He successfully drove a wedge between our lead pastor and me. I went sixteen weeks without having any communication or a meeting with my pastor.

After months of this man's scheming, the senior pastor made the decision to fire me. He made the announcement on a Sunday morning service that there would be significant changes in the youth group. The pastor's two brothers told me I would be fired on Monday.

God moved miraculously, and our lead pastor changed his mind. God spoke to him somewhere between that announcement during Sunday morning service and our scheduled meeting Monday morning. When we met together he said, "John,

God sent you to us and you will not leave until He says it is time for you to go."

Six months after this, my boss's behavior was exposed, and he was instantly released from the church team. What he was involved with was much more severe than most of us had imagined.

During this season, not only was I navigating this and other external battles, but also many internal battles like I'd never faced before. Again, I wondered if there was something wrong with me, so I began to confess every sin I could recall that I might have committed, but there was no relief from the attacks or my dryness.

One day in the midst of trying to figure out exactly what sin it was that I had committed, the Lord said to me, "You are not in this desert because you have sinned; I'm preparing you for the change that is coming." This was the "new wine" I described in Chapter 5.

After I had spent almost a year going through this desert, the Lord impressed on me to go on a food fast. After several days of fasting, a prayer came from my lips that my ears heard after mouth said it. The cry from my heart had bypassed my mind. I passionately cried aloud, "Lord, it doesn't matter if I am in the middle of the desert where there is no one or if I am preaching to millions, I'll do the same thing in both places. I will pursue Your heart!"

All of a sudden, bells sounded off inside and I saw what He was doing! "God, that is exactly what You have been doing in me," I said. "You have brought me to the place where I see You as my inheritance and my first love, not the ministry or anything else. So when the change comes, I won't make an idol out of it. I won't leave You as my first love and love the ministry instead of You. My heart will stay right."

Then I remembered what God said about David:

But God removed Saul and replaced him with David,
a man about whom God said, "I have found David son
of Jesse, a man after My own heart. He will do everything
I want him to do." (Acts 13:22)

Let me restate this important fact—King Saul never went through a wilderness experience. He seemed humble in the beginning—hiding in the baggage from the prophet when he was named king. But after a few rounds of success, his impurities began to surface. He won a huge battle, but he'd done it his way and disobeyed God's orders. If that wasn't enough, he then built a monument to himself. This was only the beginning of the plethora of ungodly behavior that would surface. He eventually was destroyed by the impurities that were never addressed.

There are two conditions that will expose what's inside of you. Refining fire, as already discussed, is one. The other is success. However, success exposes the impurities to everyone around you, but you may still be blind to them. In their early days, many ministers would not permit the refining fire to purify them. Yet, not unlike King Saul, they are called and eventually enter a position of ministry. Sadly, however, they never had the proper preparation. So, when success causes their impurities to surface, this success eventually leads to the demise of what they were called to do.

Saul loved his "ministry" to the point of killing in order to keep it. David was not a man after a throne; he was a man after the heart of God. While in the wilderness, David found his true source of joy; it was none other than God Himself. Twice, David had a chance to kill Saul to get the throne, and he was encouraged to do so by the men with him. If David's motives had been the same as Saul's, he would have killed for what was promised to him by God through the prophet Samuel.

There are men and women today who will slander, gossip, or lie to get what God has promised them—think of the irony of that! They are like Saul, willing to do almost anything to get or keep their inheritance. God is looking for the "Davids" who have a heart after Him, not a position, influence, money, or fame. The reworking of the old wineskin is the deepening of the character of God within you and me. It is the character of God that can contain the pressure of the new wine of the Spirit (His anointing and presence). Character is developed by seeking the One we desire to follow.

"So, how long will it take?" you may ask.

Here's my answer: "The time required shouldn't matter to you; just keep digging until the water flows." There will be many times when the answer is not found in one session of prayer. You will have to pick up again in the next prayer time—and, perhaps many prayer times after that.

When I lived in Dallas and was serving as an assistant to the head pastor and his wife, a dear friend of mine—he was an assistant pastor on the church team—and I used to pray together nearly every morning. We would come into that room at 7:00 a.m. and pray, and could often sense God's presence and His moving on our behalf. But there were many times when 8:30 a.m. would arrive (when the work day started), and we would have to leave and go to our office. We would almost feel frustrated, because there had been absolutely no breakthrough . . . no waters of refreshing. The wells were not yet opened!

The next morning, we would come in and pick up almost exactly where we'd left off. This would go on sometimes for two days, other times three days, and one time I remember it taking a week for us to receive any water! However, when the breakthrough came, the power and refreshing were ours.

As I travel to churches across America, I encounter many Christians who have allowed their wells to be plugged up and have settled comfortably into that state. The alarming fact is that I sense it is the majority—not the minority—who are in this condition. What would happen if these people stirred up the heavenly gift in them and allowed it to be released? Lives would be changed, families would be changed, churches would be changed—America would be changed!

The gift of God is lying untapped in too many. But even if the wells seem plugged, the Spirit is waiting.

Keep digging! You will find fresh water in the wilderness!

11

PREPARE THE WAY OF THE LORD

Adversity is always unexpected and unwelcomed. It is an intruder and a thief, and yet in the hands of God, adversity becomes the means through which His supernatural power is demonstrated.

—Charles Stanley

"I tell you the truth, the Son can do nothing by Himself. He does only what He sees the Father doing."

—John 5:19

The desert, or wilderness, is the place where the way of the Lord is prepared, the place where every mountain is made low and every valley exalted. Isaiah describes this in such a memorable fashion in this well-known passage:

> Listen! It's the voice of someone shouting,
> "Clear the way through the wilderness
>   for the Lord!
> Make a straight highway through the wasteland
>   for our God!
> Fill in the valleys,
>   and level the mountains and hills.
> Straighten the curves,
>   and smooth out the rough places.
> Then the glory of the Lord will be revealed,
>   and all people will see it together.
> The Lord has spoken!"
>
> A voice said, "Shout!"
>   I asked, "What should I shout?"

"Shout that people are like the grass.
  Their beauty fades as quickly
  as the flowers in a field.
The grass withers and the flowers fade
  beneath the breath of the LORD.
  And so it is with people.
The grass withers and the flowers fade,
  but the Word of our God stands forever." (Isaiah 40:3–8)

What does this mean exactly to those of us who may be in a wilderness season now?

In the body of Christ, we all have responsibilities that the Lord has assigned to us. But before God can release us to accomplish them, we are in need of some testing and training in the wilderness where our flesh is crucified. There, too, we learn to wait on the Lord, to be still until we hear His voice and understand what He is doing, so we can obediently accomplish His will.

I want to share more of my personal story to illustrate how the journey through the wilderness may involve less than a direct route from departure to destination, including some puzzling detours and unplanned rest stops.

In 1979, as a college student at Purdue University, I was born again in my college fraternity. Four months later, I was filled with the Holy Spirit, and God began to prompt me concerning the ministry. Believe me, ministry was nowhere on my radar—I wanted nothing to do with it. All the ministers I had met growing up were not men I desired to become like. I know it was judgmental, but I viewed them as kind of "out of it," having weird kids and living in deteriorating houses. I learned later, of course, that my impressions were warped—in fact, there were many sharp ministers who had great kids and lived in decent homes! But, as a young believer, I thought that in order to be a minister meant suffering an odd life or ending up in Africa living in a hut and not wearing shoes.

I grew up in a small town of 3,000 people. The only ministers I knew there were my Catholic priest (that wasn't an option for me, because they can't get married), and another pastor of a small church. He had two kids my age who were weird, and when I'd go to their house, something about it smelled terrible! One time I went there and the odor was so awful, I held my breath as much as I could until I made an excuse to leave! So you can understand why I wasn't very interested in the ministry. I didn't want to be a priest and didn't want weird kids and a smelly house. I also did not want to go to Africa as a missionary and end up in a shack.

My plans at the time were to complete my studies of mechanical engineering at Purdue, and then get an MBA from Harvard. After that, I would enter corporate America and rise up the executive ladder, make a lot of money, and give offerings to my church to support the ministry. These were my plans, and I avoided God's whispers to me concerning the ministry. (There would've been nothing wrong with this plan, but it wasn't God's plan for my life.)

Four months later on a Sunday morning, I was in church listening to the pastor's sermon when the Spirit of God delivered a sterner message to me: "I have called you to preach! What are you going to do about it?"

This time I heard clearly and responded, "Lord, even if I end up shoeless in Africa in a grass hut, I will preach, I will obey You!"

(God has His way of getting our attention. I had already been counting the cost in previous months during His smaller nudges.) Now fully aware of what I was saying "yes" to, I was prepared to please Him no matter the cost!

The Lord began preparing me. The fire inside me began to burn; I began telling my fraternity brothers about Jesus and many got saved. About a year and a half later, I started a Bible study in the fraternity, and students came from all over the campus. Every week, new people were giving their lives to Christ, getting healed, and finding freedom.

I had totally flipped my priorities! Now my desire to preach was so strong that I wanted to quit my mechanical engineering major at Purdue and go to Bible school. My reasoning? Why study calculus and physics when I am called to preach, and people are dying and going to hell? Jesus could return soon, so I must go to the harvest fields as soon as possible.

One night, as I was doing the homework that I now despised, I looked from my engineering book to the Bible on the shelf. I'd had it! I threw my thermal dynamics textbook against the wall. I'd made up my mind—I wasn't going to wait any longer! I would quit school and go to Bible college.

I called a man who was discipling me—he was a Purdue re-searcher and a very close friend. I boldly stated, "Don, I'm leaving and going to Bible school!"

He wisely answered, "Why don't we go for a walk tonight and pray about it?" We did and God spoke to me, "In My appointed time you will minister. . . . Finish your studies in engineering."

At a later time, as I was struggling to figure out how the Lord could ever send a small-town boy to the nations of the world, I heard Him say, "Who designed and ordained this ministry you are called to, you or Me?"

"You," I said.

"Don't you think I am more concerned about this ministry coming forth than even you?" That statement got my attention.

So, I calmed down and finished my engineering degree. Upon graduating, I was hired by Rockwell International as a mechanical engineer on a U.S. Navy project. I settled into my new job and found a great church. A year later, Lisa and I were married.

I had joined the church as a single man and had served in any capacity of need. This continued after we were married. I ushered, was a part of our prison ministry, taught the pastor's children tennis, and helped in many other areas. The church also had a Bible school, so I attended night sessions.

Two years later, the church hired me to assist the senior pastor and his family. I told the pastor and other leaders that I only could commit to one year because I was called to preach. My job was to wash and fill their cars with gas, shine the pastor's shoes, run errands, pick up their children from school, give swimming lessons to their two preschoolers, take care of visiting ministers, and many other tasks. I ended up staying for four-and-a-half years, not just one.

Seven years now had elapsed since I'd said "yes" to the call of God. In college, watching all those students being saved, healed, and delivered, I had thought that full-time ministry was just days away. I had no idea about the process God would put me through.

During this period when I served the church, I tried unsuccessfully three times to get into full-time preaching. As I flew back to Dallas from Asia (after the third try to see if that was where God wanted me), I was reading the Gospel of John when I came to a verse that jumped right off the page: "God *sent* a man, John the Baptist" (John 1:6). I heard God say to me, "Do you want to be *sent* by John Bevere or do you want to be *sent* by Me?"

"I want to be sent by You."

And the Lord said, "Good, because if you are sent by John Bevere, you'll go in John's authority, but if you are sent by Me, you will go in My authority!"

After this, I settled down and focused on where God had placed me. However, after some time, the unrest returned. The wilderness training wasn't complete for that season; rather, it was still in process.

Had God put me on a shelf for those seven years until some position opened up? No! A thousand times no! I had been brought to that wilderness in order to develop godly character . . . that *His way* might be *prepared*. My character needed maturing so that I might function well in the ministry position I was called to. I would eventually learn that with every spiritual promotion, first must come the preparation for that level.

Forget Serving in Your Own Strength

No matter how good our intentions might be, without God's involvement, we can do nothing of eternal value—even in Jesus's name! The Lord Himself says, "'I tell you the truth, the Son can do nothing by Himself. He does only what He sees the Father doing. Whatever the Father does, the Son also does'" (John 5:19). What a statement! Jesus, the incarnate, anointed Son of God, said *He* could do *nothing* of any ultimate value on His own. I'll share a few examples of what I mean:

Jesus loved Lazarus and his two sisters, Martha and Mary, who lived in Bethany. Lazarus became very ill. Here's what happened next:

> So the two sisters sent a message to Jesus telling Him,
> "Lord, Your dear friend is very sick." But when Jesus heard
> about it He said, "Lazarus's sickness will not end in death.
> No, it happened for the glory of God so that the Son of
> God will receive glory from this." So although Jesus loved
> Martha, Mary, and Lazarus, He stayed where He was for
> the next two days. (John 11:3–6)

Even though Jesus was the Messiah, He still had very close friends. He loved Lazarus and enjoyed time with this family. However, we see that Jesus did nothing for two days after hearing of his friend's illness. Why didn't He go immediately to Bethany? The reason is that He had not received His orders from God. Jesus waited obediently until the Spirit of God gave the order to go. Then Jesus went.

The Lord revealed to me once that if Lazarus had been one of my friends, I would have driven immediately to his house and laid hands on him, without even thinking of asking the Spirit for His direction. Unfortunately, many of us have this mentality. We assume that since God is always with us, we don't need to ask for guidance in situations like this. But we should pause and be sensitive to God's Spirit. *God* knows what He wants, and if we wait to get His instruction or heart on a matter, He will tell us what to do.

We may have thought that, even without the Spirit's leading, if we lay hands on the sick, God is obligated to heal them at that moment. If this is true, then shouldn't we go to all the hospitals and empty them?

In some instances, the Bible reports that Jesus "healed them all," but this was not always the case. For instance, why didn't Jesus heal all the sick, blind, lame, and paralyzed people at the pool of Bethesda when He healed just one man who had been crippled for thirty-eight years (John 5)? Could it be the Spirit of God didn't lead Him to heal the others?

In another instance there was a man, lame from his mother's womb, who was left daily at the gate of the temple. Surely Jesus must have passed him each time He entered the temple. Why didn't Jesus heal him? *Because His Father hadn't instructed Him to do so.*

Later, after Jesus ascended to heaven, Peter and John on the way to the temple—by the leading of the Spirit—healed this man, causing a revival to break out (Acts 3).

When Jesus ministered, there was no set formula: some He spit on, some He laid hands on, others He simply spoke to. For another, He made mud balls and put them in his eye sockets. Still others He sent to the priests—and the list goes on. There is such surprising variety because Jesus only did what He saw His Father doing! God knew the perfect timing and manner in which each individual could receive healing.

This is what God wants for all His servants . . . to bring us to the place where we will do only what we see Jesus do and under His leading, not what we think or want to happen. Jesus says in John 20:21, "'As the Father has sent Me, so I am sending you.'" Jesus did nothing outside His Father's leading. In the same way, we must follow Jesus's example. We must live like Him, being led by the Holy Spirit, walking as only He can lead us. This requires our flesh to be submitted to the Spirit of God—the Spirit of Christ. And the optimum training ground for this Spirit-led life is the wilderness. This challenging environment is where the way of the Lord is prepared.

God said to Moses after forty years of wilderness training:

> "Now go, for I am sending you to Pharaoh. You must lead My people Israel out of Egypt." But Moses protested to God, "Who am I to appear before Pharaoh? Who am I to lead the people of Israel out of Egypt?" God answered, "I will be with you." (Exodus 3:10–12)

Now let's compare this to what God said about people who sent themselves:

> "I have not sent these prophets, yet they run around claiming to speak for me. I have given them no message, yet they go on prophesying. . . . I am against these false prophets. Their imaginary dreams are flagrant lies that lead My people into sin. I did not send or appoint them, and they have no message at all for My people. I, the LORD, have spoken!" (Jeremiah 23:21, 32)

Ouch, that stings. None of us wants a message like that from the Lord.

At age forty, Moses was not able to help or *profit* the children of Israel when he first attempted to deliver them, because *God had not yet sent him.* Even with all the great education, leadership skills, and wisdom Moses had gained in Egypt, without God's support and timing, Moses could not fulfill what *he knew* God had called him to do. His vain effort only resulted in the death of one Egyptian oppressor. Even though his intentions were noble, this initial attempt to accomplish his mission did more harm than good. After forty years of backside desert training, a new Moses emerged who would do nothing except what God told him. Now at God's appointed time, under Moses's leadership, an entire army ends up at the bottom of the Red Sea. That is the difference between our strength and God's strength—an entire army compared with one soldier.

John the Baptist trained thirty years for a ministry that lasted only six months, yet Jesus said John was the greatest prophet born of woman.

There you have it! God can do more in six months through a man or woman *sent by Him* than someone else working hard *in their own strength* for sixty years.

It is what Jesus explains: "'I tell you the truth, the Son can do nothing by Himself. He does only what He sees the Father doing. Whatever the Father does, the Son also does . . .'" (John 5:19).

Here again are Isaiah's words:

Listen! It's the voice of someone shouting,
"Clear the way through the wilderness
    for the LORD!
Make a straight highway through the wasteland
    for our God!
Fill in the valleys,

and level the mountains and hills.
Straighten the curves,
    and smooth out the rough places.
Then the glory of the LORD will be revealed,
    and all people will see it together.
    The LORD has spoken!"

A voice said, "Shout!"
    I asked, "What should I shout?"

"Shout that people are like the grass.
    Their beauty fades as quickly
    as the flowers in a field.
The grass withers and the flowers fade
    beneath the breath of the LORD.
    And so it is with people.
The grass withers and the flowers fade,
    but the Word of our God stands forever." (Isaiah 40:3–8)

God is saying that the wilderness is where the way of the Lord is prepared. The way of the Lord is not the strength of man. He says that the pride of flesh shall be made low, the humble (those who wait on the Lord) exalted, the crooked (deceitful, inaccurate, insincere) places made straight, and rough (unloving, rude, harsh) places made smooth.

As a college student, a newly converted follower of Jesus, I had received many blessings and found "success" ministering to others, but there were mountains in my life to be made low and rough and crooked places to be made smooth and straight. God knew that I needed some wilderness time to smooth out some flaws.

In any wilderness period, it is so important to allow God to have His way with us. While I was in the position of serving my pastor in Dallas, the Lord spoke to me one day and said, "John, don't miss what I want to do in you today by only looking for the preaching ministry of tomorrow." Honestly, I so badly wanted to preach that I viewed this phase of my life as a waste of time.

You don't need to fall into this trap! Realize that God is not

---

Survival Tips for Your Journey

#11 Keep Your Bags Packed

Although I would never recommend it, when your wilderness stay has stretched on for what seems forever, you might decide to unpack your suitcases and settle in. Trust me—when God decides to move, He can do it turbo style. Look at Joseph; it appeared that he would be in the dungeon the rest of his life and with no warning, he was promoted to his God-given dream in one day! Yes, that's right—just one day!

I was in a wilderness and it was feeling like what seemed a forty-year stay in the making. Then, out of the blue, the Lord told me that I would leave my current position and start traveling and speaking. Change didn't happen immediately, but when it did happen, it came like a whirlwind. And I was ready to roll into the next season of my calling. My bags were packed.

wasting time! He is the one who *redeems time*! Realize that where you are presently is a vital part of where you are going. It is your training arena. It is the process of going from the promise to the promotion—it is fulfillment. Let Him worry about how it will all work out and come together . . . you just flow with Him! He is God, the Author and Finisher. All we are to do is trust Him and obey what He is showing us *today*!

Every time I thought I had figured out how He was going to establish me in the preaching ministry, He would kindly say, "John, you have just figured out another way it will not happen!" This was true—He brought the ministry to me in a totally unexpected way. God brings us to a place of contentment (not complacency) so we can live fully in the present.

Do Things God's Way

When God gives His authority and power to a man, the mightier the authority and power bestowed, the greater the judgment for not obeying the Spirit of the Lord. God did not judge Moses at forty when he did things his own way, because God's authority and power were not yet on him. However, later this was not the case. While in the wilderness of Zin, the people contended with Moses and complained about the place to which he had brought them. They were thirsty and wanted water. So God told Moses what to do:

> And the LORD said to Moses, "You and Aaron must take the staff and assemble the entire community. As the people watch, speak to the rock over there, and it will pour out its water. You will provide enough water from the

rock to satisfy the whole community and their livestock."
(Numbers 20:7–8)

God told Moses to speak to the rock and it would give the
water. But read what Moses did:

> Then Moses raised his hand and struck the rock twice with
> the staff, and water gushed out. So the entire community
> and their livestock drank their fill. But the LORD said to
> Moses and Aaron, "Because you did not trust Me enough
> to demonstrate My holiness to the people of Israel, you will
> not lead them into the land I am giving them!" (Numbers
> 20:11–12)

Notice God gave the water to the millions who watched. Wow!
Water from a rock—who has heard of such a powerful miracle in
the twenty-first century? So, even though Moses had disobeyed
God's instructions on how to release the water from the rock, the
profound miracle still occurred. The water was for the people, in
response to their need. God did not hold back the water from the
people in order to punish Moses. But there was a consequence:
Moses was prevented by God from leading the people into the
Promised Land.

This is a perfect example of how the supernatural anointing
of God is for the needs of the people, not to exalt the one who
has the gift! Possibly, Moses was frustrated with the people and
a little frustrated with God because of having to pastor such difficult people. Moses struck the rock, as he had done previously
in the wilderness of Sin (Exodus 17:1–7). Or perhaps Moses had

become comfortable with his ability to lead; maybe he now felt God would honor whatever he deemed best. Once again he had done something his own way, but this time the consequences were considerably greater. Moses had walked in the power and might of God; all his strength was from his dependency on God. Now for Moses to act independently of God before the people brought swift judgment.

That is why James 3:1 says, "My brethren, let not many of you become teachers, knowing that we shall receive a stricter judgment" (NKJV). The greater the responsibility or glory, the greater the judgment.

The wilderness prepares us to walk in the power and glory of the Lord without the resulting judgment for disobedience. In the dry desert experience, pride is lowered and humility is exalted. The truly humble man walks as Jesus walked, crying, "I will not do anything unless I see the Spirit of the Lord do it. I am nothing in my own strength and ability."

Is it possible that the reason God has withheld the manifestation of His glory and power from so many in the church today is to protect us from greater judgment? I believe it's in the wilderness where He is stripping the flesh from the spirit to cause us to cry out for and listen to Him. Then when His glory manifests, we will bring honor to His name by doing things only *His way*!

Hear the voice of the Spirit. Let Him show you how He wants you to conduct the work He has for you. See and hear what the Lord is doing and saying.

> I will climb up to my watchtower and stand at my guard-
> post. There I will wait to see what the LORD says and how

He will answer my complaint. Then the LORD said to me, "Write My answer plainly on tablets, so that a runner can carry the correct message to others. This vision is for a future time. It describes the end, and it will be fulfilled. If it seems slow in coming, wait patiently, for it will surely take place. It will not be delayed. Look at the proud! They trust in themselves, and their lives are crooked. But the righteous will live by their faithfulness to God." (Habakkuk 2:1–4)

The prophet said, "I will watch to see what God will say unto me." One of the ways the Spirit of God speaks is through vision. Jesus said He only did what He *saw* the Father doing. Habakkuk said he would write what he saw and run with what he saw at the appointed time. He went on to say that the soul that is proud (lifted up) is not upright (that is the man who does not wait on the Word of the Lord, but runs without the vision of what God is saying). But the just shall live by his faith, not by another's faith!

Faith comes by hearing what God is saying and then obeying it. This is why God brought the children of Israel into the wilderness, ". . . to teach you that people do not live by bread alone; rather, we live by every word that *comes* from the mouth of the LORD" (Deuteronomy 8:3). Notice He said "comes" and not "came."

We are encouraged, "See that you do not refuse Him who speaks [present tense]. For if they did not escape who refused Him who spoke on earth, much more shall we not escape if we turn away from Him who speaks from heaven" (Hebrews 12:25 NKJV). But never forget, what He speaks will always line up with Scripture.

However, searching the Bible to back up what *you* think should be done is not God's way. Jesus could have said to Himself, "I am anointed to heal the sick, so I'll go at once to lay hands on Lazarus as I have done before." Instead, He waited for the Spirit of God to move, then He moved.

The wilderness is where God brings us to teach us that any attempt to do something for Him, apart from His leading and ability, is an exercise in futility. When we truly learn that the flesh can do nothing worthy of eternal value, then we are ready to execute those dreams and plans He has entrusted to us. The wilderness is all about preparation—it is the process to the promise fulfilled. Let us follow Jesus's example, being led by the Spirit to do things *God's* way and not *our* way.

12

VICTORY IN THE WILDERNESS

Our sorrows are all, like ourselves, mortal. There are no immortal sorrows for immortal souls. They come, but blessed be God, they also go. Like birds of the air, they fly over our heads. But they cannot make their abode in our souls. We suffer today, but we shall rejoice tomorrow.

—Charles H. Spurgeon

When people do not accept divine guidance, they run wild.
   But whoever obeys the law is joyful.

—Proverbs 29:18

T he wilderness is a place we visit, not our ultimate destination! If handled correctly, you will experience victory in the wilderness and move beyond its borders!

I'd been in my passion-drained wilderness as a youth pastor for what seemed to me way too long. I was beginning to wonder if any change would come to my struggle. Then one day, shortly before the trouble began with my direct boss who tried to discredit and fire me, the Spirit of God showed me that change was coming. That was when God revealed that I would be "sent to churches and cities from the east coast to the west coast of America; from the Canadian border to the Mexican border; to Alaska and Hawaii . . ."

But, as I mentioned before, it didn't happen the next day or even that week! In fact, six months passed without any additional confirmation. Then, one day my senior pastor walked into a meeting and said that the Lord had shown him that one of his pastors (there were eleven of us on staff) would be traveling full-time soon and would no longer serve on our church's staff. "John Bevere, that man is you," he said.

Yet still more time passed (another six months, to be exact)—more time walking through the desert. Then, in a period of only three weeks, I received seven invitations to preach—one was an hour from the Canadian border, one on the East Coast of Florida, another an hour's drive from the Pacific Ocean, and one was on the Mexican border! I walked into my pastor's office to ask him what to do about them, and he laughed and said, "John, I told you the Lord had shown this to me. Looks like your time is here."

Soon after (January 1990) during a dedication service, the pastor laid hands on Lisa and me, and we have been traveling full-time ever since! It's safe to say that we have seen *much* (and I can't overemphasize the word "much") more fruit in our lives because we waited on God's timing, rather than launching ourselves when I thought I was ready.

I long to see the same results for you in your calling. This is why, as a sixty-year old man who dearly loves God's people, I've been as raw, honest, and open with you as possible. I want you to succeed in your destiny! So, let me offer some final important thoughts.

The Right Purpose and Destination

Our focus must be on the purpose of God, not on the resistance we face that tries to keep us from pressing on. We must have the right vision before us if we are to finish at the right destination! It would be a terrible thing to run a race and cross the wrong finish line! It would be a disaster to aim a gun at the wrong target and hit it!

The Pharisees were very zealous and diligent, but their purpose was self-seeking. They did not have the proper vision; therefore, they missed the mark.

What is the destination and purpose of God for us as His people? He says in Ephesians 1:11 that we have been "... predestined according to the purpose of Him who works all things according to the counsel of His will" (NKJV).

Many people get tripped up when they hear "predestined" or "predestination." In order to understand this idea, we must break apart the word and look at it by the root and prefix. The prefix "pre" simply means "before" or "prior to the beginning." The root "destination" means "where you will end" or "the finish line." Putting the two together, it means "to set the finish line before the start." Ephesians 1:11, therefore, shows us that God set a destination for mankind—prior to creating us—that would fulfill His purpose.

Romans 8:28–29 says:

And we know that all things work together for good to those who love God, to those who are the called according to His purpose. For whom He foreknew, He also predestined to be conformed to the image of His Son, that He might be the firstborn among many brethren. (NKJV)

Our destination, which God planned before time began, was for us who love God to be conformed to the image of Jesus Christ. Everything done in life or ministry should be toward this goal or end! God's number one purpose for creating you was not just so you could join a successful ministry team, give millions of dollars to the kingdom, be a known artist, or have any other career goal. It wasn't even to heal the sick, pursue humanitarian relief efforts, rescue sex-trafficked victims, get people free from addictions, or win the lost to Jesus. As noble and godly as all these pursuits are, we must realize that there have been many who have done those things but didn't cross the finish line. The reason they didn't finish well is because their focus was on the ministry and not the goal or heart behind the ministry!

Now the question must be answered: "What was the purpose of God in predestining us to be conformed to the image of Jesus Christ?" The answer is simple—because He loved us and desired fellowship with us so "that in the ages to come He might show the exceeding riches of His grace in His kindness toward us in Christ Jesus" (Ephesians 2:7 NKJV).

Lisa and I have a dog named Lexi. She is delightful, playful, and fun. However, we can only communicate with her on a limited level. It's frustrating at times that I can't have more of a conversation with her. On the other hand, it's a completely different scenario with our sons. As they have become mature, we've enjoyed amazing interactions with them. They've added so much to our lives. This is why God created us. He doesn't desire the lower-level of fellowship that I tolerate with Lexi. He wants sons and daughters to communicate with at a heart level.

That was His purpose right from the beginning. When He created man and placed him in the Garden, the Lord walked and had fellowship with Adam because of His love for him. One of Adam's descendants caught hold of the purpose of God, and it is recorded of him that "Enoch walked with God; and he was not, for God took him" (Genesis 5:24 NKJV). The writer of Hebrews says that ". . . he [Enoch] had this testimony, that he pleased God" (Hebrews 11:5 NKJV). Why did Enoch please God? Was it because he had a great ministry of some kind? No, it was because he walked with God and had close fellowship with Him.

Everything that God has done in the past, is doing now, and will do in the future will be for that reason. So, the purpose of the wilderness is to point us in the direction of being conformed to the image of Jesus Christ.

If we lose sight of God's purpose for us, we will cast off restraint and regress spiritually. As a church, when we lose sight of the purpose of God, we dry up, shrinking into an institution driven by the things of the world. We emphasize results—larger numbers and bigger buildings—rather than making disciples in the image of Christ (Matthew 28:19).

Let's look again at Proverbs 29:18: "Where there is no revelation, the people cast off restraint" (NKJV).

The restraint God is speaking of keeps us from settling for the low-level call, which is anything short of being conformed to His image and likeness. It is the restraint that keeps us from being satisfied until we are conformed to His image and behold Him face to face and see His glory revealed. It is the restraint that keeps us from accepting anything short of His perfect will. This restraint will keep us from being at ease and doing things the way the world does, from doing things in the way of the flesh.

In speaking of vision, Jesus said, "The lamp of the body is the eye. If therefore your eye is good, your whole body will be full of light. But if your eye is bad, your whole body will be full of darkness" (Matthew 6:22–23 NKJV). He is not speaking of our physical eye, but the eye of the heart, or the way we perceive things.

The way you perceive things in your heart is the way you will become: "For as he thinks in his heart, so is he" (Proverbs 23:7 NKJV).

The way you see the circumstances in which you find yourself will determine how you come through them. The twelve spies who went to gather intelligence on the Promised Land all saw the same sights—the same fortified cities, the same giants, and the same armies of the Canaanite nations. However, two of them—Joshua and Caleb—saw it in a totally different way than the other ten. The two perceived it the way God saw it, and the ten perceived the Promised Land through the eyes of natural experience or their own abilities and strengths. Because their eyes were bad, the rest of their behavior (or as Jesus said, "their whole body") was also bad. They spoke with their mouths and responded with their actions in a manner contrary to the will of God, and He said that their report was "evil" or "bad";

> "Now tell them this: 'As surely as I live, declares the LORD, I will do to you the very things I heard you say. You will all drop dead in this wilderness! Because you complained against Me, every one of you who is twenty years old or older and was included in the registration will die. You will not enter and occupy the land I swore to give you. The only exceptions will be Caleb son of Jephunneh and Joshua son of Nun.'" (Numbers 14:28–30)

What caused the ten spies to give a report that would cause them to never see what God had promised them? It was how they perceived what was before them—it wasn't prophetic vision; it was natural vision. What they saw was what they reported.

In order to come through the wilderness victoriously, we must see things the way God sees them. The children of Israel already had been complaining for more than a year before God sent the spies into the Promised Land. Their perspective was already bad, and all restraint had been discarded. So, by the time God allowed them to see the land that flowed with milk and honey, they rejected the good things they saw. Instead they focused on the giants in the land.

Those who see only the wilderness (and the hardships associated with it) will die in their wilderness. Those who keep their eyes set on the Promiser and the vision He has set before them will come through the wilderness as sanctified warriors, ready to take and live in the Promised Land set before them to the glory of God.

> Therefore we do not lose heart [faint or cast off restraint].
> ... For our light affliction, which is but for a moment, is
> working for us a far more exceeding and eternal weight
> of glory, while we do not look at the things which are
> seen, but at the things which are not seen [perceiving
> things the way God does]. For the things which are seen
> are temporary, but the things which are not seen are eter-
> nal. (2 Corinthians 4:16–18 NKJV)

The length of time and the sufferings experienced in the wilderness—compared with what will be gained—are considered a light, momentary challenge. Of course, when you are in the middle of the wilderness, seeing the experience as not that big of a deal is hard, unless you have the vision of what comes after you exit the desert.

When I was in the middle of dry times in my past, they sure didn't seem like a "moment." Sometimes I thought, *Is this going to end? Is what God promised ever going to come to pass?* That is when I quickly had to cast down those thoughts and encourage myself in the Lord. I would remember the prophecies previously made concerning me, and by them wage strong warfare (see 1 Timothy 1:18). The prophecies were the vision of God for my life, as He revealed it to me by His Spirit through His Word.

The soul is the battlefield in the wilderness. The soul consists of your intellect, emotions, and will. The *will* is that part of your soul that decides whether you choose God's way or the way of the flesh—if you will see things as God does or if you will give attention to your affliction in the wilderness. Peter writes, "Dear friends, I warn you as 'temporary residents and foreigners' to keep away from worldly desires that wage war against your very souls" (1 Peter 2:11).

It all comes down to who is your center of focus—the Lord or you? The fleshly desires that battle in your intellect and emotions will focus on selfish interests. These will draw you away from your godly vision, for God's way is not the way of self, but the way of *denying* self.

The gospel that has been preached and accepted by many today has been a gospel of ease to the flesh. Many of the mainstream messages don't encourage us to crucify the flesh, but rather to comfort and satisfy the desires that actually fight against the end goal of being conformed to Jesus Christ. Often the focus is "What can God do for me?" rather than "What does He desire of me?" The gospel of ease does not emphasize the reality of the sufferings involved in pursuing Christ. It has caused many to settle down into a complacent lifestyle. Such a gospel has not equipped believers to be the soldiers of God.

The apostle Paul touches on this theme in writing to his disciple Timothy:

Endure suffering along with me, as a good soldier of Christ Jesus. Soldiers don't get tied up in the affairs of civilian life, for then they cannot please the officer who enlisted them. (2 Timothy 2:3–4)

Because of this "gospel of ease," if we experience resistance or hardship we seek an escape route, rather than facing the difficulty and pressing through it. The vision that is birthed by the teaching of the gospel of ease is not the "heavenly or prophetic vision," but rather a "selfish vision."

Paul also writes:

"And so, King Agrippa, I obeyed that vision from heaven. I preached first to those in Damascus, then in Jerusalem and throughout all Judea, and also to the Gentiles, that all must repent of their sins and turn to God—and prove they have changed by the good things they do. Some Jews arrested me in the Temple for preaching this, and they tried to kill me." (Acts 26:19–21)

There are many visions in the world, but only one "vision from heaven," which is the will of the Father! Notice what Paul says, "Some Jews arrested me in the Temple for preaching this, and they tried to kill me." He was pursuing the heavenly vision and experiencing great resistance. If he had believed the gospel of ease, as many have preached and believe today, he would have

Survival Tips for Your Journey

#12 Take Good Notes

As I'm writing this, I am now in my last year of my fifties—how did that happen?! Looking back, I now realize that my times of wilderness were the greatest times of growth in my life, though at the time I felt like I was receding, not advancing. That's why our old friend Job said, "'I go forward . . . He's not there . . . . But He knows the way that I take; when He has tested me, I shall come forth as gold'" (Job 23:10 NKJV).

Truthfully, I would estimate that ninety percent of what I've written—now in twenty books—I learned, not in times of abundance, but in the dry times spent in the wilderness. So my advice to you—take good notes when you are in the desert! What you learn in these seasons will become a great strength to others (including the older you). And who knows . . . maybe your experiences will turn into a book someday!

My friend, I want to prophesy over you right now! Pay careful attention to what I have to say: *In God's timing, He will do something in your life that is profound and will impact the lives of many people. That is, if you allow Him to fulfill His purpose for your wilderness season. Many people are going to be impacted, and you will rejoice throughout all of eternity when you see the fruit of your obedience. My friend, you are going to come forth as gold; tested, strong, and true.*

never seen the vision fulfilled. He would not even have made it to King Agrippa, because much earlier he would have sought the way of escape from all the resistance he was experiencing.

Jeremiah was another man of the Bible who was pursuing the heavenly vision and as a result of his obedience, was experiencing a lot of verbal and mental persecution. He became weary of it one day and began to complain a little. He said, "'Why does the way of the wicked prosper? Why are those happy who deal so treacherously?'" (Jeremiah 12:1 NKJV)

God did not respond sympathetically. He said, "'If you have run with the footmen, and they have wearied you, Then how can you contend with horses?'" (Jeremiah 12:5 NKJV). In other words, "Jeremiah, if you are getting weary of the devil's foot soldiers, what are you going to do when you face the devil's cavalry?"

A War Has Battles

We must remember that there are no great victories without great battles. It did get tougher for Jeremiah. He went from being verbally abused to being thrown in prison, and still later he was dropped in a dungeon and left to die. However, God eventually delivered him from all his afflictions and persecutions.

The battles that most in the body of Christ are experiencing today are mental attacks, not the physical persecution that Paul experienced. What will we do if the resistance changes? The afflictions we endure presently must strengthen us to handle greater battles in the future.

The wilderness is a boot camp and training ground for future battles. Just as we send soldiers to boot camp to prepare them for war, even so God sends His enlisted soldiers to the wilderness to prepare them for what they are called to do in building His kingdom. The greatest obstacles soldiers have to overcome in boot camp are their fears, weaknesses, and discouragement. Likewise, the greatest battles we experience in the wilderness are in the realm of the soul.

One of the biggest battles we face is *discouragement*. One day while I was in prayer, the Lord asked me what was the opposite of *courage*.

My response was, "Fear, of course."

He whispered, "It's discouragement." I had never looked at *dis-courage* in this light! This immediately showed me the "why" behind Joshua being told eight recorded times to "be strong and of good courage" (Numbers 13:20; Deuteronomy 31:6, 7, 23; Joshua 1:6, 7, 9, 18). The Lord knew this would be one of his greatest challenges. Discouragement occurs in deserts or battles from focusing on ourselves rather than on God and our mission.

The enemy's purpose is to get your focus on you, which is what he tried to do with Jesus in the wilderness. Jesus was hungry from not eating for forty days, and the devil came and said, "If You are the Son of God, command that these stones become bread" (Matthew 4:1–11 NKJV). The temptation was to use the power of God apart from God's way to provide what His flesh desired. We must remember that when God gives a gift, it comes with a serious responsibility not to misuse it, but to administer it as He desires. God was going to make sure Jesus's needs were met, but it would be done His way. When the devil left, angels came and ministered to Jesus.

Again, let's look at what Jesus says concerning His ministry:

So Jesus explained, "I tell you the truth, the Son can do nothing by Himself. He does only what He sees the Father doing. Whatever the Father does, the Son also does" (John 5:19).

Notice the word "sees." Jesus did nothing apart from the will of God.

When in dry times, one of our temptations will be to do it our way, rather than waiting on God's way. This might be using God's power to get something before God's timing. Can you imagine a soldier in a battle not fighting according to his officer's orders? This could result in serious damage, both to the soldier and to those fighting with him. In boot camp and all of his training, that soldier learns to obey orders so that he will not foolishly risk harm for himself and others during battle.

It is important that we not forget what heaven has revealed to us. There will be times when we think, *I have got to have an answer now!* Or, *I have got to make a move now; if I do nothing, everything will fall apart!* If God does not seem to be saying anything to you, that does not mean He isn't *speaking* to you! What I mean is that God is very involved with us in many ways. In this instance, the message He is "communicating" is, "You don't need to do anything now." In those situations, we must *wait* on the Lord and not force things:

Wait patiently for the LORD. Be brave and courageous.
Yes, wait patiently for the LORD. (Psalm 27:14)

If we focus on our needs and not on Him, discouragement and heaviness will set in. We cannot get distracted and focus on our "light affliction." Instead, we must keep our eyes on the exceeding and eternal weight of glory that is being worked for us in the affliction (2 Corinthians 4:17).

This is the joy set before us that must capture our vision.

The Joy Set before Us

My brethren, count it all joy when you fall into various trials, knowing that the testing of your faith produces patience. But let patience have its perfect work, that you may be perfect and complete, lacking nothing. (James 1:2–4 NKJV)

Joy is a spiritual force that gives us strength to endure afflictions and trials. Notice the Word says, "Count it *all* joy," It does not say, "Count it part joy and part sorrow." We are not to mix up a combination of joy and sorrow in our hearts. Look at it like this: You can have a chain with ninety-nine links of joy and just one link of sorrow. That chain will only be as strong as that one link. It has to be one hundred parts joy and zero parts sorrow in order to find the strength you need for your given situation.

You and I know it is easy to "count it all joy" when everything is going great. But that is not what the text says. The time to "count it all joy" is in the time of trials—wilderness, persecution, hardship, affliction, and any other adversity. God says this because He knows that ". . . the joy of the LORD is your strength" (Nehemiah 8:10). It's the joy of being in a close relationship with Him that strengthens us.

My wife and entire family—sons, daughters-in-law, and grandchildren—bring me joy! There are times when I'm away from home and pull up a picture of them. This never fails to bring joy to my heart. It also brings strength to me.

That is what Nehemiah was saying to his men. They were going through a tough time, so Nehemiah cried out, "Don't sorrow over this adversity—get your eyes on the LORD. Because when you draw near to Him, joy will fill your heart and it will be strength to you" (my paraphrase).

Praise will cause your focus to turn from you to the Lord. In the midst of trials, it is easy to lose sight of the ability of God because of the intense pressure we face. David wrote the majority of his Psalms in the middle of trials. By praising God, he was able to stay strong in really adverse circumstances.

In Isaiah 61:3, God says that He gives us, ". . . the oil of joy for mourning, the garment of praise for the spirit of heaviness" (NKJV).

I remember a very dry time when this verse meant so much to me. I was at home alone and a heaviness set in. I picked up my Bible to read and could barely do it. So I began to pray, and that was even worse. Inside I could sense that the Spirit of God was saying to me, "Turn on one of your praise CDs." So I went to the room where our sound system was located and turned on some praise music and began to sing along. More was needed so I started to *try* to dance before the Lord. I was so heavy in heart that it was like dancing through liquid lead. Needless to say, I was struggling.

When the medley of songs was over, I felt compelled to play the same set again. The second time through, I began to hear what I was singing. All of a sudden, I saw a glimpse in my heart of Jesus on the throne and His great love. Joy began to spring up into my soul, and I began to dance completely unhindered. I noticed that my eyes had gotten off of myself and onto the greatness of Jesus. For the next thirty minutes, I sang and danced and ran around our little home like a wild man. The heaviness had lifted, and I had life and strength flowing out of me where there had been none just thirty minutes earlier.

As I was praising Him, my focus turned back toward Him. I experienced what Isaiah writes, "With joy you will drink deeply from the fountain of salvation!" (Isaiah 12:3) and through the joy of the Lord, I began to draw strength from the wells of salvation.

Praise helps us keep our eyes on the joy set before us, rather than on the circumstances that surround us.

> Therefore, since we are surrounded by such a huge crowd of witnesses to the life of faith, let us strip off every weight that slows us down, especially the sin that so easily trips us up. And let us run with endurance the race God has set before us. We do this by keeping our eyes on Jesus, the champion who initiates and perfects our faith. Because of the joy awaiting him, He endured the cross, disregarding its shame. Now He is seated in the place of honor beside God's throne. Think of all the hostility He endured from sinful people; then you won't become weary and give up. After all, you have not yet given your lives in your struggle against sin. (Hebrews 12:1–4)

Jesus endured the greatest trial that anyone ever *has* faced or ever *will* face by keeping His eyes on the joy set before Him, which was the resurrection that followed the crucifixion. It was the glory that would follow the obedience of His suffering and ultimately bring many sons and daughters into His kingdom—which includes you and me!

That is the way it is for us who follow in His steps. Beyond denying self and crucifying the flesh awaits *resurrection life*. Beyond the sufferings of the flesh is the needed maturity to produce a closer relationship with Jesus! Beyond the hardship of the desert is great glory! Paul writes, "For I consider that the sufferings of this present time are not worthy to be compared with the glory which shall be revealed in us" (Romans 8:18 NKJV).

God's glory will be revealed in the church prior to His return. The magnitude of it will be so great that it will draw cities and nations of people to salvation. Never before will the earth have seen such a demonstration of His power, as will be revealed in those followers of Christ who have allowed God to purify them. This outpouring of His Spirit, which will lead into the great harvest, will need no promotion by man. It will be promoted by God's power and glory!

> Dear friends, don't be surprised at the fiery trials you are going through, as if something strange were happening to you. Instead, be very glad—for these trials make you partners with Christ in His suffering, so that you will have the wonderful joy of seeing His glory when it is revealed to all the world. (1 Peter 4:12–13)

Again, what is the joy set before us? It is His glory being revealed in those of us who have suffered as a result of obedience to Christ. Notice that the extent to which you suffer is the extent to which you should rejoice, knowing that the greater the resistance, the greater the glory!

Lose Your Life

My friend, do not stop your pursuit of God when resistance comes! I know that He will lead you into tough situations in life, because the greater the battle, the greater the victory for the kingdom and for you. But in the midst of these battles, always keep this guarantee before you:

> God keeps His promise, and He will not allow you to be tested beyond your power to remain firm; at the time you are put to the test, He will give you the strength to endure it, and so provide you with a way out. (1 Corinthians 10:13 GNB)

No matter what trial looms, you have the power to get through it and get through it with success and glory. Otherwise you wouldn't be facing it; God wouldn't permit it!

If you *love* your life, you will quit in the tough places. You will end your pursuit and settle down to a fruitless lifestyle.

Revelation 12:11 says, "And they have defeated him by the blood of the Lamb and by their testimony. And they did not love their lives so much that they were afraid to die."

Those who are more concerned about themselves than the will of God are those who love their own lives, and Jesus says, "'If you try to hang on to your life, you will lose it. But if you give up your life for My sake, you will save it'" (Matthew 16:25).

The only way to endure what lies ahead in the days to come is to lose your life. I want to exhort you to continue to press on "until at last the Spirit is poured out on us from heaven. Then the wilderness will become a fertile field, and the fertile field will yield bountiful crops" (Isaiah 32:15).

The wilderness is not the place where we are to lay down our weapons of war and give up! It is the place where we are to be strong, bold, and courageous to do the will of the Lord. It is the place we are to submit ourselves to God and resist the devil steadfastly.

If you are in the wilderness now, God has brought you into this place so that you may know what is in your heart. Many times what I initially thought was the devil's temptations were really some hidden areas of my life that needed to be submitted to Christ.

As you continue your pursuit of the heavenly prize, remember these words:

Now thanks be to God who always leads us in triumph in Christ . . . . (2 Corinthians 2:14 NKJV)

Who shall separate us from the love of Christ? Shall tribulation, or distress, or persecution, or famine, or nakedness, or peril, or sword? Yet in all these things we are more than conquerors through Him who loved us. (Romans 8:35, 37 NKJV)

But thanks be to God, who gives us the victory through our Lord Jesus Christ. (1 Corinthians 15:57 NKJV)

Do not quit in your pursuit of Him. Do not give up. Keep the vision that He's given you, no matter how the circumstances appear.

It seemed hopeless for Joseph in the pit and later in a foreign country when he was thrown into the dungeon. His life appeared over. How could he possibly have any future? Remember, though, "Humanly speaking, it is impossible. But not with God. Everything is possible with God" (Mark 10:27).

Even so with you—no matter how tough it gets, remember, "'Anything is possible if a person believes'" (Mark 9:23).

Keep your eyes on the joy set before you, which is His glory manifested in you. This will give you the strength to overcome the trials you face. Continue to seek Him with all your heart, and believe what He speaks to you by His Spirit through His Word. If you do, you will experience victory in the wilderness.

> Now to Him who is able to keep you from stumbling,
> And to present *you* faultless
> Before the presence of His glory with exceeding joy,
> To God our Savior,
> Who alone is wise,
> Be glory and majesty,
> Dominion and power,
> Both now and forever.
> Amen. (Jude 1:24–25 NKJV)

DISCUSSION QUESTIONS

If you're reading this book along with *The Wilderness* study or course (which is a great idea!), I recommend that you watch each week's video lesson and unpack the corresponding discussion questions as a group. The video lessons will parallel and amplify major themes from this book, so it's ideal for all participants to both watch the lessons and read the book.

Enjoy!

Lesson 1

Read Chapter 1

1. What is the difference between the omnipresence and manifest presence of God? Why is it helpful for us to understand the difference?

2. Why is it so important to be able to discern the season we are in and know whether we are in a wilderness season or not?

3. Why do you think Satan uses wilderness seasons to tempt us to willfully sin or give up on our faith?

4. Why would God allow us to extend a wilderness season?

Lesson 2

Read Chapters 2 and 3

1. The wilderness has several purposes. From the seven purposes mentioned in this lesson, which one resonates with you the most and why?

2. Why do you think obedience to God in the wilderness produces spiritual growth?

3. The wilderness is a time of self-discovery. What are some of the things you've learned in the wilderness about yourself and your walk with God?

4. How have you learned to find your strength in God during this time of humbling?

Lesson 3

Read Chapter 4

1. Between a promise and its fulfillment, there is always a process. Why do you think this process is important?

2. How have you seen the process of the promise working in your life?

3. Why do you think God gives you a promise before you experience a process?

4. Why is it important to have a promise from God for your life rather than just a five-year plan?

Lesson 4

Read Chapters 5 and 6

1. How does comparing the lives of Saul and David help us understand the importance of God refining us through the wilderness?

2. Refining gold makes it more flexible, and God's refining of us makes us more tender to Him. Describe what it means to be more tender toward God.

3. When God's refining process reveals hidden sin or weakness, what should our response be?

4. How does the refining process position us to reveal Jesus more clearly?

Lesson 5

Read Chapter 7

1. Why does God hate complaining? What does complaining currently look like in your life?

2. What is the difference between the complainers in Malachi and the complaining of Jeremiah? Why was God upset with one group, yet answered Jeremiah's complaints?

3. Judgment means decision, not condemnation. When judgment begins in the house of God, He is deciding who is worthy of His service. What do you think God looks for when making this decision?

4. God is looking for vessels fit for service. How would you describe the difference between being called and being chosen?

Lesson 6

Read Chapter 8

1. What was your initial response when you heard that suffering is a gift? How did your perspective change by the end of the lesson?

2. God will not allow you to be tested beyond what you can handle. How does this encourage you?

3. God will not leave you at your current strength. What does this teach you about God's plan for your life?

4. God allows us to enter trials today that will simulate the pressures we'll face tomorrow. What has God spoken to you about your future that helps you make sense of the pressures you feel in your trials now?

Lesson 7

Read Chapter 9

1. Following God doesn't always make sense. Why is it difficult to trust God when He "violates" the traditional ways of doing things?

2. How do you feel when God doesn't act according to your timetable? What pressures and temptations do you feel when God's promise seems delayed?

3. How have you seen this truth evident in your life: *Whatever is birthed in the flesh must be sustained by the flesh*? How does this differ from what God births through you?

4. What gives you an assurance that you are following God's path for your life?

Lesson 8

Read Chapter 10

1. The wilderness is a place where God reveals Himself. Why then does God also seem distant in this season?

2. What does it look like to pursue God first, rather than His blessings?

3. Why is it dangerous when your promise or calling becomes more important to you than God Himself?

4. When you see the pattern of how God revealed Himself to the heroes in Scripture, how does it change what you expect to receive from your wilderness season?

Lesson 9

Read Chapter 11

1. Why is it important for us to be mindful of where we go for comfort, especially during spiritually dry times?

2. When we dig deeper in prayer and Scripture, especially when we don't feel like it, how does this strengthen our spiritual roots?

3. How are you encouraged knowing that the greatest attack against your harvest comes immediately before the harvest manifests?

4. Why does meditating on God's faithfulness transform a wilderness season?

Lesson 10

Read Chapter 12

1. How has a wilderness prepared you for a change of season?

2. Why is change difficult? What is often your biggest hurdle adjusting to change?

3. What stood out to you the most from the process of renewing a wineskin? Why did this stand out to you?

4. To lay hold of the new, we must let go of the old. What are things you need to let go of in order to embrace the new?

APPENDIX
Salvation, Available to All

If you confess with your mouth that Jesus is Lord and believe in your heart that God raised Him from the dead, you will be saved. For it is by believing in your heart that you are made right with God, and it is by confessing with your mouth that you are saved.

—Romans 10:9–10

God wants you to experience life in its fullness. He's passionate about you and the plan He has for your life. But there's only one way to start the journey to your destiny: by receiving salvation through God's Son, Jesus Christ.

Through the death and resurrection of Jesus, God made a way for you to enter His kingdom as a beloved son or daughter. The sacrifice of Jesus on the Cross made eternal and abundant life freely available to you. Salvation is God's gift to you; you cannot do anything to earn or deserve it.

To receive this precious gift, first acknowledge your sin of living independently of your Creator, for this is the root of all the sins you have committed. This repentance is a vital part of receiving salvation. Peter made this clear on the day that five thousand were saved in the Book of Acts: "Repent therefore and be converted, that your sins may be blotted out" (Acts 3:19 NKJV). Scripture declares that each of us is born a slave to sin. This slavery is rooted in the sin of Adam, who began the pattern of willful disobedience. Repentance is a choice to walk away from obedience to yourself and Satan, the father of lies, and to turn in obedience to your new Master, Jesus Christ—the One who gave His life for you.

You must give Jesus the lordship of your life. To make Jesus "Lord" means you give Him ownership of your life (spirit, soul, and body)—everything you are and have. His authority over your life becomes absolute. The moment you do this, God delivers you from darkness and transfers you to the light and glory of His kingdom. You simply go from death to life—you become His child!

If you want to receive salvation through Jesus, pray these words:

God in Heaven, I acknowledge that I am a sinner and have fallen short of Your righteous standard. I deserve to be judged for eternity for my sin. Thank You for not leaving me in this state, for I believe You sent Jesus Christ, Your only begotten Son, who was born of the Virgin Mary, to die for me and carry my judgment on the Cross. I believe He was raised again on the third day and is now seated at Your right hand as my Lord and Savior. So on this day, I repent of my independence from You and give my life entirely to the lordship of Jesus.

Jesus, I confess you as my Lord and Savior. Come into my life through Your Spirit and change me into a child of God. I renounce the things of darkness which I once held on to, and from this day forward I will no longer live for myself. But by Your grace, I will live for You who gave Yourself for me that I may live forever.

Thank You, Lord; my life is now completely in Your hands, and according to Your Word, I shall never be ashamed. In Jesus's name, Amen.

Welcome to the family of God! I encourage you to share your exciting news with another believer. It's also important that you join a Bible-believing local church and connect with others who can encourage you in your new faith. Feel free to contact our ministry (visit MessengerInternational.org) for help finding a church in your area.

You have just embarked on the most remarkable journey. May you grow in revelation, grace, and friendship with God every day!

GOD, WHERE ARE YOU?!

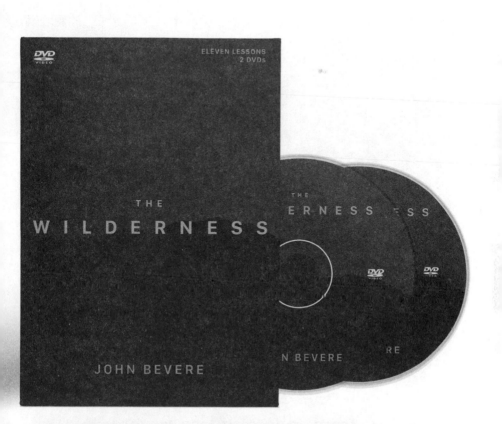

 **COURSES**

Get exclusive courses from John and Lisa Bevere

Visit MessengerCourses.com to learn more

BOOKS BY JOHN

Available in study format

MESSENGER INTERNATIONAL

Messenger International exists to develop
uncompromising followers of Christ who
transform our world.

Call: **1-800-648-1477**

Visit us online at: **MessengerInternational.org**

Connect with John Bevere:

JohnBevere.com